THE COMPROMISE OF 1850

Problems in American Civilization

UNDER THE EDITORIAL DIRECTION OF

George Rogers Taylor

THE COMPROMISE OF 1850

EDITED WITH AN INTRODUCTION BY

Edwin C. Rozwenc

v.27

Problems in American Civilization

READINGS SELECTED BY THE
DEPARTMENT OF AMERICAN STUDIES
AMHERST COLLEGE

D. C. HEATH AND COMPANY: Boston

INTRODUCTION

VERY few who read the history of the American Republic can fail to be stirred by the great political debate which accompanied and followed the war with Mexico. The Mexican War was a victorious war, yet it was a war that created great tensions in American politics. Anti-slavery men in the North opposed the war as an expansionist conspiracy on the part of the slaveowners of the South. Henry David Thoreau spent a day in jail for refusing to pay taxes that might support such an unjust enterprise and then wrote *Civil Disobedience* to explain his philosophy of freedom. James Russell Lowell assailed the territorial gains of the Mexican War in *The Biglow Papers* with such verses as:

> They just want this Californy
> So's to bring new slave states in
> To abuse ye, an' to scorn ye
> An' to plunder ye like sin.

In the Congress, anti-slavery Democrats and Whigs rallied behind a proposal known as the Wilmot Proviso. When President Polk asked for an appropriation of two million dollars for the purchase of territory from Mexico, Representative David Wilmot of Pennsylvania sought to attach to the appropriation bill a proviso to the effect that "neither slavery nor involuntary servitude shall ever exist" in any territories so acquired. David Wilmot became a hero overnight in the North and every northern legislature except one endorsed

his Proviso. The Proviso was defeated in the Congress, but it became a burning political issue in the campaigns after 1846. Indeed, in 1848, a third party calling itself the Free Soil Party was formed by a coalition of old abolitionists who had supported the Liberty Party in 1840 and 1844, and "Conscience Whigs" and "Barnburner Democrats" who accepted the free soil principles of the Wilmot Proviso.

At the same time, debates continued to rage in the Congress over the issue posed by the Wilmot Proviso. As these arguments became more heated, sectional positions began to harden, particularly at the extremes. Northern anti-slavery men took the position that Congress had the moral duty to prohibit slavery in the territories of the United States; freedom was in harmony with our national purposes, slavery was a sectional institution which must be contained in the states where it already existed. Southern fire-eaters countered with the claim that Congress had no power to prohibit slavery in the territories, instead it had a plain constitutional duty to protect slavery in the territories held by the states in common.

The debate became more than an indoor sport in the halls and taverns of Washington during the first year of Zachary Taylor's administration. The gold discoveries in California and the spectacular rush of the "forty-niners" from every part of America to the stream beds on the slopes of the Sierra Nevada soon created a population that qualified California for admission to the Union even before Congress had been able to set up a territorial government for the newly acquired territory on the Pacific coast. Undismayed, the Californians chose to leapfrog the territorial stage by summoning a convention, drafting a state constitution which prohibited slavery, choosing a governor and legislature under the new constitution, and then confidently awaiting a ratification of this *fait accompli* from the Congress. By this action, the die was cast for the members of Congress; decisions could no longer be postponed concerning the territorial questions which had filled the air with such fulgurous rhetoric in the years since David Wilmot had become a hero.

And so the stage was set for the great debate of 1850. It was a debate in the grand style, dealing with fundamental questions concerning the nature of the Union and the Constitution. It was a debate in which the sections, North and South, sought to re-examine the basis for their reciprocal relations in the Union. It was a debate which engaged the old and the new generations: grand old political leaders like Clay, Calhoun, Webster, and Benton and rising young political leaders like William Henry Seward and Stephen A. Douglas. The days of debate were full of color and excitement; craggy brows, graveyard coughs, baleful stares, nervous maiden speeches, stentorian declaiming, ladies in the gallery, commotions without the Senate Chamber—all were there.

Yet, despite the historical uniqueness of the activities associated with the Compromise of 1850, we may also view the Compromise as a case study of the problem of preserving a democratic consensus in an expanding and complex commu-

nity. Democracy is sometimes defined as a political system which subordinates the rule of force, in the struggle of groups and interests, to the rule of opinion. And the rule of opinion requires a willingness to accept the continuous co-existence of conflicting opinions. In a democracy, then, men may cherish their dogmas, but not to the extent of destroying other men for their contrary dogmas.

This, then, is the question which a historian (or a sociologist or political scientist) must ask himself concerning the Compromise of 1850: Did the Compromise really accommodate the competing beliefs and dogmas of the groups and sections which were involved in the political conflict that followed the Mexican War? The arrangement of materials in this volume is designed to give the reader an understanding of this controversy in Congress and in the country at large in 1850.

The first selection sets the stage for the reader with a well-rounded summary of historical events relating to the Compromise of 1850. This is an account of "the crisis" of 1850 written by Avery Craven as a part of his objective study (from the angle of the South) of the coming of the Civil War.

The next five selections are crucial for the study of this problem. They are lengthy selections from the speeches of Henry Clay, Thomas Hart Benton, John Calhoun, Daniel Webster, and William Seward delivered in "the great debate" during the first session of the 31st Congress. These speeches indicate the differing political strategies that were proposed to the Congress and the reasoning and value systems on which they are based.

The three selections which follow represent differing historical interpreta-

tions of personal roles and policy proposals in "the great debate." The selection from Schouler is a favorable inter-
pretation of the ideas and behavior of
Zachary Taylor, William Henry Seward,
and Thomas Hart Benton. The selection
by Richard Current is a sober appraisal
of "the great compromisers," especially
Daniel Webster, which cautiously char-
acterizes the political strategy of the
compromisers as successful. The selection by Herbert Agar praises the political theory of John Calhoun although not
necessarily the devices by which "the
rule of the concurrent majority" was to
be implemented.

The next two selections take the reader into a close examination of the com-
plicated parliamentary maneuvers which
finally produced the legislation of 1850
and provide him with additional data
concerning the response to the Compromise by groups and individuals in
both the North and the South. The selection by George Fort Milton reveals the
important role played by Stephen A.
Douglas in the Senate in lining up Democratic support for separate bills after
the failure of Clay's "Omnibus Bill."
Allan Nevins, in the second selection of
this group, shows that the Compromise
was accepted with enthusiasm—but also
with conditions and reservations in the
North and the South.

The final selection by Dorothy Fosdick
entitled "Ethical Standards and Political
Strategies" moves us from the level of
the concrete historical situation to the
level of abstract theory with a penetrat-
ing analysis of the difficult human problem of relating ethics and politics. Dr.
Fosdick's essay offers us sharper analytical tools and additional logical categories
for our reflections about the Compromise
of 1850.

In truth, the historian who ventures to

inquire into the Compromise of 1850
needs his best analytical equipment because the subject bristles with difficult
questions at every turn. If we accept the
theory that democracy sanctions the continuous coexistence of conflicting social
beliefs and subordinates the rule of force
to the rule of opinion, then we must ask
ourselves first of all, was there really "a
crisis" in 1849–1850 which required ex-
traordinary measures of compromise?
John Calhoun, for example, gave full expression in the debate to the values and
beliefs of the South, but were these beliefs and values threatened by forcible
destruction or merely by the vigorous expression of contrary dogmatisms? Was
Thomas Hart Benton realistic or un-
realistic when he questioned the necessity of any elaborate legislative log-rolling under the name of compromise? Was
Senator Benton being bombastic or pene-
trating when he asserted that the salvation of the Union "lies not in the contrivances of politicians or the incubations of committees," but "in the hearts
of the people"? What shall we say of
Schouler's conclusion that Zachary Taylor's simple policy for the admission of
California was the most practical approach to the territorial problem because it depended least upon Congress
and, consequently, that agitation of the
territorial question might have been adjourned for twenty years?

Did the compromisers really accommodate differences in fundamental values
and beliefs of the competing groups in
American society? Were the compromisers classic prototypes of leaders skilled
in the art of democratic compromise,
or did they merely attempt to appease
the holders of one fanatical minority
opinion (after their inability to achieve
leadership in the South had been demonstrated) only to inflame the holders of

another fanatical minority opinion in the North? Did the Compromise of 1850 settle "the angry issue" of slavery in the territories or did the compromisers help to create dangerously ambiguous and conflicting ideas about the meaning of the territorial settlement which planted the seeds that were to bear bitter fruit in the reopening of the territorial question in 1854?

Applying the analytic categories of Dorothy Fosdick, the historian may also ask: Who of the proposers of policy and makers of political decisions in 1849–1850 were attempting to apply an "absolute ethic" to politics? Was Seward, for example, an exponent of ethical absolutism as Webster seemed to suggest, or does not his insistence that democratic policy should always seek the alternative which moves toward the higher good put him in the class that Dorothy Fosdick calls "neo-Machiavellian"? How should Webster, Clay, and Calhoun be classified in this kind of analysis of political strategies? Is it possible to characterize Stephen A. Douglas as anything other than a "pure Machiavellian"?

The readings in this volume can provide only tentative answers for many of these questions. Indeed, it is not only the student with a bookkeeping mind who may discover that he will emerge from this experience with more questions than answers. If so, the never-ending process of human inquiry will be served well and a few may even be provoked to try to add more to our historical knowledge of the Compromise of 1850. Others may find lessons in the human thoughts and actions of 1850 which may be instructive for present day problems of the American political community, some of which still involve deeply rooted differences of habit and thought in the South.

[The sentences by Allan Nevins in the Clash of Issues on page xii are from *Ordeal of the Union* by Allan Nevins (Vol. 1, pp. 257, 290–291); copyright 1947 by Charles Scribner's Sons; used by permission of the publishers.]

CONTENTS

The Clash of Issues

Of Clay's compromise proposals, Thomas Hart Benton said:

It is proposed to make the admission of California a part of a system of measures for the settlement of the whole slavery question in the United States. . . . I am against the mixture, and that for reasons which apply to the whole in the lump, and to each separate ingredient in the detail.

I am against it in the lump.

To which Clay replied with a statement of his political philosophy:

I go for honorable compromise whenever it can be made. Life itself is but a compromise between death and life, the struggle continuing throughout our whole existence, until the Great Destroyer finally triumphs. All legislation, all government, all society is formed upon the principle of mutual concession, politeness, comity, courtesy; upon these everything is based. I bow to you today because you bow to me.

However, Seward reminded Clay that:

There is another aspect of the principle of compromise which deserves consideration. It assumes that slavery, if not the only institution in a slave state, is at least a ruling institution, and that this characteristic is recognized by the Constitution. But *slavery* is only *one* of many institutions there—*freedom* is equally an institution there. Slavery is only a temporary, accidental, partial, and incongruous one; freedom, on the contrary, is a perpetual, organic, universal one, in harmony with the Constitution of the United States. . . .

Many years later, James Schouler, an historian, offered these observations:

Of all these famous Senatorial speeches, Seward's was by far the most profound, and worthiest of being read in a calmer age. It was full of thought and humanity, and lighted up with prophetic insight. . . . Had Clay and Webster—or either one of them—stood by their president, history might have vindicated a policy against which rebellion had no just cause for appeal. Sooner or later California's admission as a free state must have been granted if she was to remain a national prize at all, and in all other respects—except the boundary issue of Texas—the territorial question might have been adjourned for twenty years.

Still more years later, another historian, Allan Nevins, wrote of President Taylor disparagingly:

> The President's plan was for several reasons quite unrealistic. . . . Taylor assumed a readiness to postpone every controversial topic save California when half a dozen were actually irrepressible. . . .

but of Daniel Webster's Seventh of March speech Mr. Nevins wrote these words of praise:

> No speech more patriotic or evincing a higher degree of moral courage had ever been made in Congress. For once Webster rose to the highest level of statesmanship. In the fierce light of history written by events during the next generation, hardly a line of his address failed to meet the test of truth and wisdom.

AN ACCOUNT OF THE HISTORICAL EVENTS RELATING TO THE COMPROMISE OF 1850

Avery Craven: THE CRISIS

THE election of 1848 only intensified the sectional conflict. The short session of Congress which convened a few weeks later was less than ten days old when the slavery issue made its appearance. Senators tried to avoid a struggle; Representatives seemed to court trouble on every possible occasion. To the last sessions of the House the issue remained a smouldering fire which broke intermittently into flame. "From morning to night, day after day and week after week," said a member, "nothing can get a hearing that will not afford an opportunity to lug in something about negro slavery. . . . Sir, I am heartily tired of this nigger business. I want a change. I beg gentlemen to remember there are some white people in this country, and that these white people are entitled to some consideration. . . . Yet, a stranger . . . on listening to the debates on this floor would consider . . . that Congress was instituted mainly for the benefit of negroes."

Dissatisfaction over political irregularity was in part responsible for this condition. The more positive attitudes taken toward slavery by both sides were a more important factor. Robinson, a Democrat from Indiana, boldly charged that slavery had determined the result of the late presidential election and that henceforth he intended to support the Wilmot Proviso regardless of party pressure. Brown of Mississippi, an equally good Democrat, complained that "thou-sands and tens of thousands of voters in the North [had] been brought to General Taylor's support on the Free-Soil issue." Hereafter he intended to vote on all occasions "to maintain the rights of the South in their broadest latitude." Extremists saw the opportunity to press issues with greater effect and to keep political waters troubled. In that spirit, Root of Ohio asked that the Committee on Territories be instructed to report a bill providing a territorial government for each of the Territories of New Mexico and California, and excluding slavery therefrom. Giddings then tried to secure an act by which the citizens of the District of Columbia, black and white, should choose between slavery and liberty. Gott of New York brought the attack to a climax by declaring that "the traffic now prosecuted in this metropolis of the Republic in human beings, as chattels, is contrary to natural justice and the fundamental principles of our political system, and is notoriously a reproach to our country throughout Christendom, and a serious hindrance to the progress of republican liberty among the nations of the earth." He offered a resolution for the prohibition of the slave trade in the District of Columbia.

Southern reaction to these efforts was quick and positive. Calhoun took the lead. He saw more clearly than others the dangers involved. More than a year earlier he had surveyed Northern attitudes and acts, and had predicted for the

Reprinted from Avery Craven, *The Coming of the Civil War* (New York: Charles Scribner's Sons, 1942), pp. 241–265. Used by permission of the author.

South a fate in comparison to which "the conditions of Poland would be a state of bliss." He had tried to stir his section to action. Benton even charged him with attempting to create issues in order to bring about secession. In August, before the short session, Calhoun had addressed a meeting in Charleston. He had measured the value of the Union against "our honor and our liberty" and declared that Southern generalship and soldiership were equal to those of the North. In closing, he had urged the calling of a Southern Convention to consider a program of action. Rhett was willing then to withdraw the state's representatives from Congress and to stand unaided and alone. Response, however, had been slow. A few local groups answered, but the legislature of South Carolina was not ready for separate action. Other Southern states had been even more conservative. In the proposals of Gott, Giddings, and their fellows, however, men of the South saw new concrete evidence of Northern aggression. If such legislation were passed, their section would indeed be reduced to the status of an inferior. Amid great excitement the Southern congressmen met in caucus and instructed a committee to prepare a statement of position. The result was Calhoun's "Address of the Southern Delegates in Congress to their Constituents."

The Address surveyed the whole unconstitutional invasion of Southern rights and concluded that aggression had followed aggression until the section could no longer remain silent. It asserted that every single provision, stipulation, or guaranty of the Constitution intended for the security of the South had been "rendered almost perfectly nugatory." It prophesied that abolition would be certain if the North were permitted to monopolize the territories, and thus acquire

a three-fourths majority in Congress. It foretold a struggle between the races which would result in the prostration of the white race. It begged for Southern unity.

Meanwhile the governor of Virginia, in his message to the legislature, had declared that if Proviso measures passed Congress, "then indeed the day of compromise will have passed, and the dissolution of our great and glorious Union will become necessary and inevitable." The legislature, in response, had reaffirmed its earlier resolutions against the Proviso and had authorized the governor to convene the legislature in extra session to consider modes of redress if the suggested legislation were passed by Congress. In South Carolina, committees of Safety and Correspondence were formed in most of the districts and parishes, and in May a state convention was held in Columbia to approve the Southern Address and to concur in the Virginia resolutions. The Florida, North Carolina, and Mississippi legislatures also took action looking toward the defense of slave interests, and meetings or conventions in Alabama, Mississippi, Tennessee, and Georgia revealed a strong sentiment in favor of cooperation and resistance. A Southern Movement had been launched.

Much extreme talk had accompanied these developments. Calhoun expressed fear that "the alienation between the two sections [had] . . . already gone too far to save the union." He saw "an increasing disposition to resist all compromises and concessions and to agree to nothing." "Disunion [was] the only alternative." J. H. Hammond found the conviction "growing rapidly . . . that the union . . . always [had] been and always . . . [would] be a disadvantage to . . . [the South] and . . . the sooner . . .

[she could] get rid of it the better." The Mississippi *Free Trader* declared "the time for talking or threatening . . . past; we must lay down our platform broadly and openly, and say to our Northern brethren, 'thus far and no further.'" The *Sumter Banner* (S. C.) insisted that "the only remedy which [would] free . . . [the South] from Northern oppression, from the Wilmot Proviso and all its evil results [was] the SECESSION OF THE SLAVEHOLDING STATES IN A BODY FROM THE UNION AND THEIR FORMATION INTO A SEPA-RATE REPUBLIC."

Conservative voices, however, could still be heard. The Whigs generally minimized the danger and even questioned the value to the South of New Mexico and California. Only two Southern Whigs supported "Calhoun's Address" in the Congressional caucus. Both Cobb and Berrien of Georgia issued minority addresses to their constituents and urged quiet and compromise. Cobb, writing to his wife, referred to Calhoun as the old reprobate, and added: "If it would please our Heavenly Father to take Calhoun and Benton *home,* I should look upon it as a national blessing." B. F. Perry, although he supported a Southern convention, wrote: "I love the Union of these States, & look upon their dissolution with horror approaching despair." The Richmond *Times* believed that nine tenths of the Southern people distrusted Calhoun's judgment and the Savannah *Republican* stated in no uncertain terms that it was not yet tired of the Union and intended to stand by it.

Northern reactions were as intense as those of the South. Political truancy became the order of the day. Blair talked of "the Free Democracy standing aloof." Others were ready to drop party leaders who did not agree with the Cleveland *Plain Dealer* that: "Rather than see slavery extended one inch beyond its present limits we would see this Union rent asunder!" Letters from the Northwest spoke of the fusion of Free-Soilers and Democrats and the rapid decline of Whig power. "Men who last fall proved the Wilmot proviso a humbug & unconstitutional," wrote one Indianan, ". . . are now hugging the proviso as a darling." Another spoke of "the bargain and sale . . . going on between locos and free soilers"; and yet another declared that "*all* factions are beginning to fraternize throughout the land." In Ohio, Chase was chosen senator over Allen by a combination of Free Soil and Democrat votes. Illinois and Indiana both replaced conservative senators with men of more pronounced Free-Soil views. The refusal of Thomas H. Benton to receive instructions from the Missouri legislature on slavery in the territories sealed his fate. Early the following year he found himself again in the company of Blair and Van Buren with free-soil his only hope of return to power. The threat made by Congressman Delano of Ohio two years before was being carried out. "Conquer Mexico," he had cried, "and add the territory but we will make it free; if not with the politicians we have now, the people of the North will bury these and send honest men in their places. If you drive on the bloody war of conquest to annexation, we will establish a cordon of free States that shall surround you; and then we will light up the fires of liberty on every side until they melt your present chains and render all your people free."

*   *   *

When the new Congress assembled early in December, 1849, sectional feeling was at white heat. In October, a

Mississippi state convention had issued a call to all the slaveholding states to send delegates to a Southern convention at Nashville, Tennessee, "on the 1st MONDAY IN JUNE next, to devise and adopt some mode of resistance to [Northern] . . . aggressions. . . ." Thoughtful men believed that this was the first step toward the breakup of the Union. Many Northerners were ready to accept it as such if that were the price required to stop the spread of slavery. "The North is determined that slavery shall not pollute the soil of lands now free . . . even if it should come to a dissolution of the Union," said an Ohio newspaper.

To make matters worse a series of events during the past year had turned some rather remote abstract questions into very immediate concrete ones. On a March morning in 1848, a San Francisco newspaper had carried the following bit of news: "Gold mines found. In the newly-made race-way of the Saw Mill recently erected by Captain Sutter, on the American Fork, gold has been found in considerable quantities." A restless people stirred. The slow westward American trek became a series of mad rushes. Eighty thousand persons reached California in one year. As many more were on their way. The Mormon, Marshall, had begun the transformation of the vague, unreal California of the Mexican treaty into a rugged social-economic reality in which ten thousand homes back east felt a close personal interest. The year 1849 quickly earned the sobriquet, the days of gold. Horizons lifted. California presented everything Western in exaggerated degree and form—greater opportunity, more rapid settlement, easier wealth. Lawlessness matched other extravagances. The frontier urge to self-government, in turn, more quickly asserted itself. Without consent or assist-

ance from Congress, the people of California met in September, 1849, and formed themselves into a state, framed a constitution, elected senators, prohibited slavery, and now stood, hat in hand, asking admission.

The year had also seen the problem of the fugitive slave greatly magnified. Since the Court had decided that federal authorities must enforce the law, some Northern states had shed their responsibility in ways which made recovery of runaways exceedingly difficult. In a few cases, citizens of such states resisted the slaveowner with impunity and accepted the abolition opinion that slavery was "a state of war, and escape from its battlefields both justifiable and meritorious." The recent publication in Virginia of Doctor Ruffner's pamphlet against slaveholding and similar writings by C. M. Clay and Thomas Marshall in Kentucky had produced in the Cotton Kingdom distrust of the border states, and had caused steps to be taken against the further importation of slaves from the border. Texas had become alarmed by the demands for the organization of New Mexico where her boundary claims had not been satisfied. She too was ready to add something to the determination, distrust, and bitterness which surrounded the gathering of the thirty-first Congress.

Trouble began at once in the House. The Democrats and Whigs were so nearly equal in number that a handful of Free-Soilers held the balance of power. The attempt to elect a speaker produced a deadlock. Cobb of Georgia and Winthrop of Massachusetts were the strongest candidates, but neither could muster the required majority as long as the Free-Soil members scattered their votes among other candidates. Day after day the voting went on. Behind the scenes pledges were demanded and bargains attempted. On the floor of the House, speakers increasingly revealed their stubborn resolve to express the tense and uncompromising attitudes of their sections. Sharp passages between members became more frequent as the days became weeks and attempts at organization failed. The votes scattered, and again concentrated. Brown of Indiana took the lead. Southerners gave him ready support. Then debate showed that he had given some assurance to the Free-Soilers regarding the appointment of committees. The price of organization was to be the Wilmot Proviso. Bedlam broke loose. Meade of Virginia declared that "if the organization of this House is to be followed by the passage of these bills [abolition of slavery in the District of Columbia and in the territories]—if these outrages are to be committed upon my people, I trust in God, sir, that my eyes have rested upon the last Speaker of the House of Representatives. . . . If these be passed, there will be but one determination at the South—one solemn resolve to defend their homes and maintain their honor." Duer of New York called him a "disunionist." "It is false," Meade retorted. "You are a liar, sir," Duer snapped back. Meade rushed toward him. Friends intervened. Even the dull reporter for the *Congressional Globe* was caught in the excitement and for once dropped his plodding:

Indescribable confusion followed—threats, violent gesticulations, calls to order, and demands for adjournment were mingled together. The House was like a heaving billow. The CLERK called to order, but there was none to heed him. Some time elapsed.

The Sergeant-at-arms of the late House of Representatives . . . now took the mace in his hand, and descending among the crowd of members held it up on high.

Cries of "Take away the mace; it has no authority here."

When some semblance of order was restored, members realized that a crisis had been reached. The mock innocence with which Wilmot had insisted that all he had demanded was a majority of fair Northern men on committees and the irritating humor with which Root had justified Free-Soil tactics now seemed out of place. Some wished to adjourn; others attempted to press an immediate election of a Speaker. Then Toombs of Georgia, a Southern conservative, who, only a few months before, had foiled Calhoun's "miserable attempt to form a Southern party," took the floor. His black, uncombed hair stood "out from his massive head," his eyes glowed "like coals of fire," and his sentences rattled "like volleys of musketry." Bluntly he went to the heart of the matter. "A great sectional question [lay] at the foundation of all these troubles." By a "discreditable trick" Northern members had attempted to gain an advantage in the formation of important committees. The interests of the South were in danger. No longer was he interested in organizing a body from whose legislation his section could hope for nothing. To organize would open the treasury to the use of one half the nation. It would bestow the territories, won by common blood and effort, upon the same half. The rights of a minority section would end. "Sir," he said, "I have as much attachment to the Union of these States, under the Constitution of our fathers, as any freeman ought to have. I am ready to concede and sacrifice for it whatever a just and honorable man ought to sacrifice . . . [but] I do not . . . hesitate to avow before this House and the Country, and in the presence of the living God, that if by your legislation you seek to drive us from the territories of California and New Mexico . . . and to abolish slavery in this District, thereby attempting to fix a national degradation upon half the States of this Confederacy, *I am for disunion;* and if my physical courage be equal to the maintenance of my convictions of right and duty, I will devote all I am and all I have on earth to its consummation."

The effect of these words was sobering. Debate was suspended for continuous voting. At length, on December 23, Cobb of Georgia was made Speaker by a plurality vote. When the result was announced, according to the *Congressional Globe,* "a slight murmur of approbation, not amounting to a distinct expression, passed over parts of the Hall."

*   *   *

Meanwhile the Senate had assembled and adjourned day after day. It contained, this session, an unusually large number of outstanding men. Henry Clay had come back. He was a bit pinched and sunken but as human and open-minded as ever. Calhoun was there—sick unto death, yet always grim and certain of the rightness of his position. The more earthy Webster, solid, stolid, and brilliant by turns, rounded out the triumvirate of great leaders who had fought together and against each other through the long years since the young nation, emerging from the War of 1812, had begun its giant strides across a continent and toward social-economic maturity. Then there was Cass, who, with good reason, thought himself the most abused man in the land, and Benton, who was about to take over that title. They were old men. Their ambitions for high office were dulled, if not completely gone. They carried many scars and a few grudges, but they loved the Union which they had helped over so many rough

places, and they could distinguish between fundamentals and the temporary emotions of the hour. They were the last gift of a passing generation to a new day.

A younger group, to whom the future belonged, showed promise of matching their elders. Some were partly seasoned, others had been thrown forward by the recent political upheavals. Seward of New York, Chase of Ohio, and Hale of New Hampshire, represented the strong Wilmot Proviso sentiment which had developed in the "Greater New England" lying north and west of the Old and rapidly spreading out along the Great Lakes. They typified the new moral attitudes toward slavery; they questioned its rights in a democracy where the Declaration of Independence formed an essential part of political dogma. They were in earnest about a better order of things. They did not intend to sacrifice principle to expediency. Douglas of Illinois represented the Older Northwest— the upland Southern, corn-and-hog area bordering the Ohio River, where economic interest suggested fairness to Southern constitutional rights along with a goodly recognition of Western needs and the national harmony necessary for their satisfaction. Douglas saw no moral issues in the conflict, only political questions which the people had a right to determine as their own well-being dictated. Davis of Mississippi and Clemens of Alabama spoke for the Cotton Kingdom, now confident of its strength and sure of its rights. They were as uncompromising of principle as their fellows from the North, as certain of the course to be followed as Calhoun himself.

The slavery issue was raised in the Senate almost at once and would not down. Every proposal seemed somehow to have a relationship to it. The question of permitting a foreign visitor to sit within the bar of the Senate brought out his anti-slavery leanings and thus led to strife over the institution itself. The customary resolutions from the legislature of Vermont, calling slavery "a crime against humanity, and a sore evil in the body politic," brought Southern senators angrily to their feet to denounce the promptings of fanaticism, and to set the stage for impassioned debate over the return of fugitive slaves and the organization of California and New Mexico. The Senate seemed about to follow the course already taken in the House. "The Southern members are more determined and bold than I ever saw them," wrote Calhoun. "Many avow themselves to be disunionists, and a still greater number admit, that there is little hope of any remedy short of it." Chase, as spokesman for the North, declared that "no menace of disunion, no resolves tending towards disunion, no intimations of the probability of disunion, in any form, will move us from the path which in our judgment it is due to ourselves and the people whom we represent to pursue."

As passions mounted Henry Clay evolved his plan. On the evening of January 21, in spite of a cruel cough, he braved the stormy weather and knocked at Webster's door. For an hour, he outlined his ideas, and Webster, deeply moved, promised support. Eight days later, the tired old man, who had earlier begged that he might be relieved from any arduous duties, rose in the Senate chamber and began his last great effort to save the beloved Union. "I hold in my hand," Clay said, "a series of resolutions which I desire to submit to the consideration of this body. Taken together, in combination, they propose an amicable arrangement of all questions in controversy between the free and slave states, growing out of the subject of Slavery." By these proposals California would be admitted as a state without Congressional action on the matter of slavery. A territorial government would be set up in the remaining part of the region acquired from Mexico without provision either for the introduction or exclusion of slavery. Somewhat restricted boundaries would be drawn for Texas, but that state would be compensated by the federal assumption of her debts. Slave trade in the District of Columbia would be abolished, but slavery itself would be allowed there as long as it continued in Maryland, or until her people and those of the District itself should accept compensation for abolition. A new and more effective fugitive slave law would be passed and the principle that Congress had no power over the domestic slave trade would be recognized.

On February 5, Clay defended these resolutions. He pleaded for moderation and for unselfish, non-partisan devotion to the Union. One by one, he took up his resolutions and asked for thoughtful consideration of each. Was there any concession to either section in the California proposal? The people themselves, not Congress, had already chosen freedom. Was the Wilmot Proviso necessary in the organization of the other territories? No. By law slavery nowhere existed, and nature, more powerful than a thousand provisos, forbade its introduction. Congress might have the power either to introduce or to exclude slavery, but patriotism demanded that the abstract principle be not pressed. The proposed boundaries of Texas were liberal and just. The assumption of her debts was a fair compensation for the loss of her right as an independent nation to collect duties. The resolutions affecting slavery and slave trade in the District of

Columbia were equally just. What more could the South ask than absolute security for property in slaves? Did not the Southern States themselves prohibit the introduction of slaves within their limits as merchandise? An effective fugitive slave act was a constitutional requirement, not a Northern concession; the acknowledgment that Congress had no right to interfere with the domestic slave trade was a concession, not a constitutional requirement!

Here was compromise. Its spirit had made possible a glorious past. Kindness, forbearance, and concessions would still enable the sections to live in happiness and peace. Disunion would solve no problems. The dissolution of the Union and war were identical and inseparable. "Conjure . . . at the edge of the precipice," Clay begged both North and South, "before the fearful and disastrous leap is taken in the yawning abyss below. . . . I implore, as the best blessing which Heaven can bestow upon me upon earth, that if the direful and sad event of the dissolution of the Union shall happen, I may not survive to behold the sad and heart-rending spectacle."

A month later Calhoun took the floor. He had been too ill to hear Clay's speech or to attend the regular sessions of the Senate. This day, wrapped in flannels, he tottered to his chair and sat with sunken eyes half closed until the consideration of the special order brought Clay's resolutions up for discussion. Then he arose, explained his inability to speak, and asked his friend, Senator Mason of Virginia, to read the speech he had carefully prepared. Another old man would make a last attempt to save the Union.

The speech which Mason read was that of a realist. "I have . . . believed from the first," it began, "that the agita-

tion of the subject of slavery would, if not prevented by some timely and effective measure, end in disunion." That measure had not come. The Union was now imperiled. The danger grew out of Southern discontent and belief that they could not, consistently with honor and safety, remain in the Union. That attitude was due to the long-continued agitation of the slavery question and to the upsetting of the equilibrium between the sections. The South had lost ground by constant surrender of territory to the North—in the Northwest Ordinance, the Missouri Compromise, Oregon, and now in the greater Southwest. The result had been a complete change in our form of government—the substitution of a consolidated union for the old confederation, and the passage of tariffs and other legislation favorable to commerce and industry and harmful to agriculture. Government by and for one section had been established.

Under such distortion the cords of the Union were snapping. The churches had already divided. The parties were now practically sectionalized. The Union could not be saved by eulogies, by Clay's proposals, or the administration's efforts to encourage the people to act for themselves in California. Congress must exercise its power in the territories and give the South justice. The South could accept no compromise but the Constitution. The North, the aggressor, must grant equal rights in the territories, cease to agitate the slavery question, faithfully observe the fugitive slave laws, and grant Constitutional amendments which would restore sectional equilibrium. If the North would not do this, California was the test question, and the Union was at an end!

Here was an ultimatum. It explained the errors of the past. It should have made clear to both North and South the necessities of the future. The nation stood at the crossroads. Vital decisions had to be made.

Back of Calhoun's position lay three basic and yet tragic assumptions, in part implied and in part stated. In the first place, he assumed, as had John Taylor, that a rural-agricultural order was the natural one; that it would prosper and dominate unless, through political trickery and legislative favors and advantages, the commercial-industrial interests were artificially built up. The South had achieved the good life and the superior order. She would have held her own and given direction to national legislation if fairness and honesty had prevailed. But she had fallen behind, was outnumbered in the House, and was threatened, by the refusal of the North to share the territories with slaveholders, with similar loss of power in the Senate. That could only mean sectional exploitation and ultimately a state of dependency. In the second place, he assumed the inferiority of the Negro—slavery as a necessity for the black man's welfare and for the safety of society. Slavery was a natural condition, and the peculiar superiority of the Southern rural-agricultural order rested in part on this institution. Without it, neither the race question nor the labor problem could be solved. Lastly, he assumed that the Fathers had established a confederate form of government, not a consolidated Union. The national government had delegated powers only; the States retained their sovereignty. True democracy was local democracy. The Constitution, as the framers intended it, was the basis of government—the rock against abuses from both sides. When the Constitution no longer protected all, and government became the agent of one interest to oppress the citizens of a state, secession was a right.

Much can be said for these assumptions. Neither history nor experience was entirely against them. Urban-industrialism and finance-capitalism have yet to prove their soundness and their superiority in producing a way of life. The evils of consolidation are only too evident in a world of dictators and Fascists. The importance of regionalism in social-economic planning is becoming more apparent every day. We have never succeeded in ridding ourselves of human exploitation, even though we have changed its forms and altered its names. The Negro has yet to achieve equality; the race question is yet unsolved. Calhoun's assumptions, however, were completely out of line with the whole trend of affairs in the United States and in the Western world of his day. His South and its values were out of date and he did not know it. The Industrial Revolution was in the ascendancy. The future belonged to the city, to the financier and the industrialist. Agriculture was declining to inferiority and dependency; farmers might no longer aspire to the status of gentlemen. A new kind of peasantry was developing. Lands were becoming a market commodity, not just a place where a home and a way of life were to be builded. Great technical changes in communication and production were cutting down space, increasing interdependence and calling for an efficiency and uniformity which only strong centralized government and dominant nationalism could give. And lastly a wave of humanitarianism and a new enthusiasm for democracy had come to help clear the way for the new economic forces. Old restraints and forms had to be broken; freedom had to be re-emphasized, opportunity exalted. New forms of human exploitation were required. Slavery, too old even when America began, had no place in a world of factories, railroads, science, and democratic symbols. Calhoun's assumptions were already invalidated by what men, a bit blind perhaps, called progress.

Daniel Webster, who spoke three days later, understood these facts. He spoke as a nationalist—as an American. The Union, he declared, could no more be peacefully dissolved than could the "heavenly bodies rush from their spheres." Secession was an utter impossibility. Extremists on both sides were wrong. Northern supremacy in population, and growth, and wealth was not the result of government action. When had the government given the North any favor comparable to the purchase of Louisiana or the annexation of Texas?—both slave areas. Superiority was the product of "the operations of time." And time, he knew, had been, and would be, with the North. She could, therefore, afford to be generous and patient. The sincere, but mistaken, abolitionist, and his harmful societies, need not press the Wilmot Proviso. There was not "within the United States, or any territory of the United States, a single foot of land" where "some irrepealable law" did not forbid slavery. Nature need not be re-enacted by legislation. Webster saw that slavery was doomed. The Fathers had expected it soon to run out. Cotton had given it temporarily a new lease of life, but time was against it. Webster was willing, therefore, in spite of his belief that slavery was a moral and political evil, to give it full constitutional rights. He would agree to support all that Henry Clay had proposed. The Union was worth temporary concessions.

Moderation and generosity characterized every paragraph of Webster's great national appeal. Yet underneath was the calm and cruel confidence which belongs to those who are in step with time. Contemporaries, at first, missed that undercurrent. New England radicals could scarcely find words in which to express their wrath. Webster was "a recreant son," misrepresenting Massachusetts, a "Benedict Arnold," "Lucifer descending from heaven," a man whose honor was dead! Southerners, on the other hand, saw in Webster's speech a guarantee that Clay's compromises would be passed. They began to hesitate. Soon a change in public opinion manifested itself, first among Southern Whigs and then among moderates throughout the section. "Our politicians have gone over to the compromisers," wrote a Virginian late in March. "We have a tolerable prospect for a proper settlement of the slavery question," was Toombs' comment. A few saw deeper. They realized that Webster had, indeed, shown a friendly spirit but that he had given no approval of the basic assumptions on which the ways of the Old South rested. They guessed that New England industrialists had good reason for applauding him.

The speech of William H. Seward, given a few days after Webster's, was even more to the point and, in some ways, more significant. Seward expressed current attitudes. He revealed future trends. He would have nothing to do with the Compromise: all compromises meant the surrender of the exercise of judgment and conscience. He would admit California at once on merit alone, and settle the other issues in like manner as a majority wished. The United States, he declared, was a consolidated Union. "The States [were] not parties to the Constitution as States; it [was] the Constitution of the people of the United States." The States had "surrendered their equality as States, and submitted themselves to the sway of the numerical majority without qualifications or checks." Sections as sections had no standing in such a government. Seward could not recognize any rights of a slave-section as such, or give it favors. The unequal, the minority, could not have the advantages of the majority, even though that minority constituted a section.

The issues before Congress were moral, Seward asserted. Slavery was a sin and Americans could not "be either true Christians or real freemen, if [they] impose[d] on another a chain [they] defi[ed] all human power to fasten on [themselves]." Southern demands for the extradition of fugitive slaves smacked of the Dark Ages. The modern conscience was against them. Human law "must be brought to the standard of the law of God . . . and must stand or fall by it." The Constitution did not recognize property in man and if it did there was a higher law than the Constitution. A Christian democracy must give freedom to its territories!

Here were the fundamental attitudes of Webster, without his spirit of tolerance, moderation, and compromise. Seward's proposals were as blunt and positive as anything Calhoun had offered. They emphasized an "irrepressible conflict" with bloodshed or submission at the end.

Fortunately for the immediate safety of the nation, not many members of Congress understood the assumptions behind Calhoun's statements and the conflict they implied with all that Seward had just uttered. Few would have been willing to follow them to their logical conclusions if they had understood. Fewer would have shared Calhoun's pessimistic realism regarding the necessity for immediate and final action. Even

Seward saw no great impending disaster and no reason for physical strife. Lesser men saw and thought even less clearly than he. Most of them expected and favored compromise after they had talked their bit. The risk they ran was that something would happen to require them to line their action up with their talk.

Thus, in spite of the fact that Davis and Chase, Brown and Wilmot, and other young leaders, expressed opinions even more dogmatic than those of Calhoun and Seward, the trend of opinion slowly turned in favor of Clay and Webster. Northern merchants anxious for peace and prosperity threw their weight in that direction; Northern conservatives were even more weary of strife than were the Southern planters. Debate went on throughout the spring and summer, but the advocates of compromise gained ground. Bell of Tennessee supplemented Clay with further resolutions. Cass and Douglas brought the force of the optimistic, democratic West to the side of peace. A Committee of Thirteen took the bills in hand. After March, a settlement was definitely in sight.

Circumstances favored. Late in March, Blair went down to the capital city to see what progress the various intrigues had made since his last visit there two weeks earlier. He hunted up his friend, "The Colo.," meaning Benton, and asked him the state of the Republic. Benton gave him interesting information regarding the old enemy, John C. Calhoun. Calhoun, he said, was "possumming of it" —feigning deathly sickness for fear of an encounter in the Senate with Webster. Some said he was writing a speech or speaking it to one of his mouthpieces to be read in the Senate. Others said that he was getting ready a constitution for the Southern Confederacy to be issued from the Nashville Convention. Only close friends were allowed to see him, but a plain man had got in a private interview and reported that he "seemed almost demented—talked of nothing but first seceding the District to Maryland—then letting Maryland go & making the Potomac the boundary & monopolizing the blessings of Negro slavery between that latitude & the tropics across the Continent." "This is his euthanasia," added Blair, "for 'tis given out that having completed this ground work he does not look to life to enjoy it—poor old man, he resolved to die in giving birth to the Southern Confederacy. . . ."

Five days later Calhoun was dead. He left behind only a fragmentary document which proposed a constitutional amendment by which he hoped the Union and Southern rights could be saved. It provided for the election of two Presidents, one from the free States and one from the slave States; either could veto all Congressional legislation.

The removal of the great South Carolinian from the scene hastened the disintegration of the Southern forces. Already a few had broken away. Foote of Mississippi, perhaps influenced by an old quarrel with Jefferson Davis, had early pledged support to Henry Clay. He had quickly dissented from Calhoun's statement that California was a test case and had forwarded the Committee of Thirteen. Blair reported in late March that "Southern men (Foote and others of his stripe) who [had] aspirations, [had] seized the occasion to secede from South Carolina instead of the Union" and had developed "quite a counter movement." Even in South Carolina many felt in regard to Calhoun's passing as did B. F. Perry, who confided to his Journal that: "I regard his death as fortunate for the country & his own fame. The slavery

question will now be settled. He would have been an obstacle in the way. . . . His death has relieved South Carolina of political despotism. Every man may now breathe more freely as England did after the death of Henry the Eighth." Preston and Poinsett agreed; Preston called Calhoun's death "the interposition of God to save the country."

President Taylor had been another obstacle to compromise. Before his election he had said that the "South must resist boldly and decisively the encroachments of the North." But once in office he proved himself considerably more the soldier than the slaveholder. He sent a personal representative to California to help establish order there; and, in his first message, he recommended to Congress the favorable consideration of the new state's request for admission. Quickly falling under Weed's and Seward's influence, he assured the people of the North that they need have no apprehension of the farther extension of slavery, and made it quite clear to Southern Whigs who called on him in February, 1850, that he would approve any constitutional bill that Congress might pass, regardless of the slavery issue, and hang any traitors who might rebel against the Union. He held out stubbornly against Clay's proposals, derided them as an omnibus bill, and advised his friends to make open, undisguised war on them.

Suddenly the whole scene changed. On July 4, the President attended patriotic exercises at the Washington Monument. He sat long exposed to a blistering sun and drank great quantities of iced water. On his return home he ate freely of cherries and followed them with cold milk. Five days later he was dead of a violent form of cholera morbus! Millard Fillmore, bitter enemy of Seward, became President!

Even more important for compromise and peace were the changing attitudes in the South. Throughout December and January it seemed that the Nashville Convention, when it met in June, might precipitate a secession movement. Radical talk was common. Democrats, as a rule, were more extreme than Whigs, less inclined to waver and more willing to threaten disunion. Yet here and there a radical Whig editor was to be found and an occasional dropping of party attitudes. In Virginia, men like Edmund Ruffin, John B. Floyd, and Beverley Tucker advocated "separation from, and independence of, the present Union." The Richmond *Enquirer* was only a trifle less emphatic. The destiny of the Union, it insisted, depended upon the present decision. Only by a strict observance of all the guarantees of the Constitution could the Union be preserved. "The only Union we love is a confederacy of equals . . . we will remain in it on no other condition." "Let us show, by assembling at the Nashville Convention, that we are prepared to meet the consequences whatever they may be. . . ."

The New Orleans *True Delta* advocated the formulation of a Southern creed, upon the violation of which the slave state delegations in Congress should retire. The *Daily Delta* averred that, should the South "be reduced to the alternative of subjection in [its] dearest right, to Northern domination, or a dissolution of the Union," her people would not hesitate to secede. Even the *Daily Crescent* was for calm but firm action.

In Georgia, Governor Towns proclaimed that further aggression was not to be endured and the legislature responded with an act providing for a state convention to consider the mode and measure of redress in case Congress should pass any of the contemplated acts affecting slavery. All Georgia, save perhaps some mountain districts in Cherokee, was ready for final resistance to the Proviso. Even in North Carolina, usually moderate, men talked of secession. "Unless there is reform, and that speedily," said the Wilmington *Commercial* (Whig), "there will be found an immense majority in all the Southern States who will very readily entertain a proposition for disunion." The North Carolina *Standard* urged a united front at Nashville and action in place of talk. A Wilmington States' rights meeting boldly declared that the South could not "yield up principle and honor, even if the maintenance of them involved the sacrifice of . . . political and individual existence, in the dissolution of the Union and the bloody consequences likely to flow therefrom."

In December, Governor Collier of Alabama recommended that the General Assembly "announce the ultimatum . . . [of the state] upon the grave question which now convulses the Union." He assured the nation that Alabama would be at Nashville "with her persecuted sisters . . . [to] present an unbroken front to insult and usurpation." For some time the Montgomery *Advertiser and Gazette* had been urging "a general convention . . . and preparation . . . to withdraw from the Union before Congress" could pass acts depriving the South of its just share of the territories. Even the moderate Mobile *Daily Register* was inclined strongly to the opinion that the causes of difference would be "pushed to the catastrophe of a dissolution of the Union."

South Carolina and Mississippi were surprisingly quiet. The call to Nashville, however, had originated with them. Their governors, Seabrook and Quitman, were outspoken States' rights men. Both accepted the possibility of secession and each made radical recommendations to his legislature. But these bodies were content to reaffirm their earlier positions and to await the Nashville Convention. The Natchez *Free Trader* and the Charleston *Mercury*, meanwhile, kept the issues before their readers. They did not openly advocate the breaking up of the Union, but neither were they willing to compromise Southern rights. Now and then, however, some local editor proclaimed it "the sacred duty of the South, enjoined by every sentiment of patriotism, honor and interest, to demand a dissolution of the Union."

Retreat from extreme positions was discernible quite early. The Whigs were not eager for a break which would rob them of the fruits of their late victory. They found it difficult not to make political capital out of the Democratic radicalism. After the first reluctant denunciation of "Northern aggressions," they hesitated. The Richmond *Republican and General Advertiser*, which in January had warned the North that attachment to the independence and institutions of the Southern States was equal to the love of the Union, was soon praising Northern enterprise and energy and denying that there were any inherent differences between the sections. Other papers took a similar stand and some began denouncing the Nashville Convention as a move "to familiarize the public mind with the idea of dissolution." The New Orleans *Daily Crescent* spoke of "the wildness, not to say silliness, of this project" and expressed a doubt whether the convention would ever meet. The New Orleans *Bee* thought it a "work of supererogation to argue against" a movement which was about to "die a natural death."

North Carolina Whigs soon fell in behind Edward Stanley, who hoped that "the citizens of Nashville [would] drive every traitor of them into the Cumberland River." Georgia Whigs, meanwhile, realizing that compromise was a possibility, opposed the holding of both state and sectional conventions. After Toombs and Stephens came out in favor of Clay's proposals, these two men were able to destroy almost completely all interest in the movement. Leading Whigs in Alabama soon began asserting that the convention should not meet unless Congress passed anti-slavery measures, and their friends in Mississippi declared they saw nothing in the admission of California as a state to warrant action. While still supporting the Nashville Convention, both groups steadily insisted on its Union purpose.

Whig opposition put the Democrats on the defensive. Gradually they too began to retreat. Long before June they were denying that any purpose of disunion was at the bottom of the movement for the Nashville Convention. All they were asking was Southern organization to match that of the North. "There are no disunionists at the South," declared the Richmond *Enquirer* on April 17. "Now we deny that any proposition or memorial for disunion has emanated from the South," echoed the New Orleans *Delta*. "Such a sad alternative has never been contemplated." The Nashville Convention was planned only as a family meeting to consult together as to the best means of "allaying the agitation, which is continually imperilling the friendly relations of these states and seriously affecting the peace and prosperity of the South." The primary object of the convention was to take steps to make the Union one of safety and permanency. "To defend the Constitution inviolate and to MAINTAIN THE UNION is the great purpose" said the Mobile *Daily Register.* "The objects of the Nashville Convention," said a Mississippi Democrat, "are to call the Northern States, the Northern people, and the Congress and Government of the United States *back to the Union* . . . and to prevent the calamities of *secession and disunion.*"

As compromise sentiment increased, interest in the convention dwindled. Outside of South Carolina and Mississippi the people showed startling indifference to the selection of delegates. The April election in Georgia was a farce and the Democrats themselves admitted that the movement was dead and buried. When Father Ritchie and his Washington *Union* decided for the compromise measures, even the Richmond *Enquirer* began to weaken. It hailed Webster's speech as a masterly production, showing "his determination . . . to do justice to the aggrieved South." Soon it was publishing articles supporting representation at Nashville primarily for the purpose of checking radicals from the lower South! More than half the Virginia counties refused to select delegates; only six of the fourteen men finally chosen were willing to go to Nashville. In Alabama, resolutions passed by county conventions made it clear that delegates were being sent to preserve, not to dissolve, the Union. A few important leaders, such as Henry W. Hilliard, questioned the right of the legislature to appoint delegates. So uncertain had opinion become by May that delegates were being asked to make known publicly whether they intended to go to Nashville or not. North Carolina and Louisiana failed to select delegates and the Tennessee legislature and many of the counties refused to act. The New Orleans *Delta* called Webster's speech a godsend—"the trident of Old Neptune,

calming the excited sea and soothing the raging billows." "Of the eight millions of people in the Southern States, not ten thousand" took any part in "the appointments of the delegates . . . who will attend the Nashville Convention," said the *Delta's* neighbor, the *Daily Crescent.*

The great Southern Convention was thus foredoomed to failure. On June 3, delegates from only nine states appeared at Nashville. The atmosphere in the Tennessee capital was anything but friendly. Most people in the South, like the editor of the *Columbus* (Miss.) *Whig,* attached little or no importance to the meeting. It was, he said, incapable of harm or of good.

The sessions of the convention brought a few fiery speeches, a series of resolutions affirming the Southern position as taken by Jefferson Davis in Congress, and an Address to the Southern people written by Robert Barnwell Rhett. Nothing was done about "the methods suitable for a resistance" to Northern aggression. These were not necessary when Congress was making such rapid strides toward compromise. The convention, therefore, adjourned to meet again in six weeks.

The resolutions passed were notable for their acceptance of an extension of the line 36° 30′ to the Pacific; Rhett's address for the lecture it gave the South against forbearance and submission, its criticism of the Clay proposals, and its final plea for Southern nationalism. Rhett believed that North and South were now two distinct peoples. The South must determine its own internal policies or perish. Neither resolutions nor address attracted much attention in the section.

The sharp changes in Southern sentiment and the complete failure of the Nashville Convention removed the last serious barrier to compromise. Measures were crowded to final acceptance during the summer months, with Stephen A. Douglas taking the lead. One by one the bills were debated, often bitterly, and ultimately passed. September saw the task completed. The Southern States must now accept or take steps toward secession.

Southern opinion on the Compromise was badly divided. There was, of course, no great enthusiasm over the admission of California, the Texas boundary, and the abolition of the slave trade in the District of Columbia, but there was a general feeling that the Compromise was the best that could be secured without radical action. Only the few were ready for that. The struggle, therefore, was completely localized again. It had to be fought out by groups within the separate states. All hope for one great sectional movement was gone. The second session of the Nashville Convention offered tragic proof of that fact. Its membership was more irregular and less official than that of the first. Its resolutions,

asserting the sovereignty of the States, the right of secession, and the unsatisfactory character of the Compromise measures, attracted little attention and had even less influence.

What the States would do was soon indicated by the action of Georgia. The passage of the California measure obligated Governor Towns to call a state convention "to deliberate, and counsel together for . . . mutual protection and safety." The election of delegates on November 26 brought a Union majority greater than any party had ever rolled up in the history of the state. When the Convention assembled in December, it drew up the famous "Georgia Platform" which said, in effect, that Georgia accepted the present Compromise but expected the North faithfully to maintain its provisions. One is reminded of an individual in one of the local meetings who violently urged resistance and who, when pressed for a program of action, said he would petition.

THE GREAT DEBATE

AN EXCHANGE BETWEEN SENATOR THOMAS HART BENTON
AND HENRY CLAY ON THE NECESSITY OF COMPROMISE

Senator Benton's Remarks

IT is proposed to make the admission of California a part of a system of measures for the settlement of the whole slavery question in the United States. I am opposed to this mixing of subjects which have no affinities, and am in favor of giving to the application of California for admission into this Union a separate consideration, and an independent decision, upon its own merits. She is a State, and should not be mixed up with anything below the dignity of a State. She has washed her hands of slavery at home, and should not be mixed up with it abroad. She presents a single application, and should not be coupled with other subjects. Yet it is proposed to mix up the question of admitting California with all the questions which the slavery agitation has produced in the United States, and to make one general settlement of the whole, somewhat in the nature of a compact or compromise. Now, I am opposed to all this. I ask for California a separate consideration, and object to mixing her up with any, much more with the whole of the angry and distracting subjects of difference which have grown up out of slavery in the United States.

What are these subjects? They are:

1. The creation of Territorial Governments in New Mexico, and in the remaining part of California.

2. The creation of a new State in Texas, reduction of her boundaries, set-tlement of her dispute with New Mexico, and cession of her surplus territory to the United States.

3. Recapture of fugitive slaves.

4. Suppression of the slave trade in the District of Columbia.

5. Abolition of slavery in the District of Columbia.

6. Abolition of slavery in the forts, arsenals, navy-yards, and dock yards of the United States.

7. Abolition of the slave trade between the States.

8. Abolition of slavery within the States.

And a non-enumerated catalogue of oppressions, aggressions, and encroachments upon the South.

This is the list of the subjects to be mixed up with the question of admitting the State of California into the Union; and I am against the mixture, and that for reasons which apply to the whole in the lump, and to each separate ingredient in the detail.

I am against it in the lump.

California is a State, and has a right to be treated as other States have been, when asking admission into the Union, and none of which have been subjected to the indignity of having their application coupled with the decision of other, inferior, and, to them, foreign questions.

I object to it upon principle—that principle of fair legislation which requires every measure to stand or fall upon its own merits, unaided by stronger measures, unimpeded by weaker ones.

I object to it on account of the nature of the subjects to be coupled with California—all angry, distracting, and threatening the Union with dissolution; while her application is calm, conciliatory, national, and promising to strengthen and augment the Union.

I object to it because California herself has objected to it. Her constitution contains this provision:

"Every law enacted by the Legislature shall contain but one object; and that shall be expressed in the title."

This is the opinion of California about mixing different subjects together in the process of legislation; and a wise opinion it is; and a wise provision it is to be put into her constitution, and worthy to be put into all constitutions, and very fit and proper to be acted upon by all legislative bodies, whether written down in their constitutions or not. California has doubtless heard of that legislative operation in the old States called *"log-rolling"*—a term which needs no definition in this assembly—and took care by a fundamental enactment—by a law of constitutional dignity, and permanent obligation, to keep it out of her own borders. And now, by what would seem to be a rebuke of her constitutional provision—a flout upon her wisdom—a satire upon her prudery—and a caution not to pretend to be better than others—it is proposed in the American Congress to perform the operation upon herself—to *"log-roll"* her, herself, into this Union!— into it, or out of it, as the case may be— as the *"rollers"* may be successful, or not, in getting their *"logs"* together.

I object to the process. I object to mixing California with anything else. I have objected in the lump; I will now take the ingredients in detail.

1. The government for the two territories. This brings up the Wilmot proviso, which is unconstitutional in the opinion of some members—inexpedient in the opinion of others—and both constitutional and expedient in the opinion of some others. It is an angry, distracting, and sectional question, with which California, for herself, has determined to have nothing to do. She has put it into her constitution, that slavery and involuntary servitude shall not exist in her borders. This settles the question of the Wilmot proviso for her, and was intended to settle it, and intended to free the question of her admission from the impediment of that question. And now, how wrong to her—how unjust—how mortifying—how unexpected and incomprehensible to her, to have the question of her admission connected with this proviso in two neighboring territories, and her admission made actually dependent upon its settlement—precedent settlement—in New Mexico and the Great Basin. She had as well have remained a territory herself, subject to the question upon her own soul, as thus to be subjected to it abroad. And better, too. There is more dignity in being tried at home than abroad—more consonance to our notions of fair trial to be tried in her own person than by proxy. After all, there is a positive incongruity and incompatibility in mixing these two questions. One is clearly constitutional. The power for it is written down in the Constitution. Congress may admit new States; and this is an application for the admission of a new State out of territory belonging to the United States; and there is no question of constitutionality in it. Not so the Wilmot proviso. Power for it is not written down in the Constitution. Its constitutionality is denied, and that by many members on this floor.

Here, then, is a coupling of an undisputedly constitutional with a strenuously disputed constitutional measure; and in voting upon them as a whole, or as mutual and dependent measures, as a system of measures, as a compromise, members may find themselves in a state of impossibility. Oaths to the Constitution cannot be compromised; and, therefore, questions of disputed should never be mixed with questions of undisputed constitutionality.

I am ready to vote for governments to the territories; and, believing in what I have alleged from the beginning, that slavery is extinct in New Mexico, and in all California, and cannot be revived in either, or in any part of either, without positive enactment, I am ready to vote them governments without any provision on the subject of slavery.

2. Texas, with her large and various questions, is the second subject proposed to be coupled with the admission of California. It is a large and complex subject, presenting in itself many and distinct points. A new State, to be carved out of her side—reduction of boundaries —settlement of the dispute with New Mexico—cession of her surplus territory to the United States: such are the large and various points which the Texas question presents. They deserve a separate consideration. Texas herself should object to this conjunction with California, as much as California should object to it with Texas. They present incompatible subjects—incongruous—and large enough each to demand a separate consideration. They are subjects of equal dignity. Each concerns a State, and States should be considered alone. But there is another objection to this conjunction, of higher order still, and which concerns this Congress, and the exercise of its powers. By the Constitution, Congress

is to admit new States: by this coupling of Texas and California, it would be Texas which would admit the new State of California. Thus: Texas has four questions to be settled, not one of which can be settled without her consent. A new State cannot be carved out of her—her boundaries cannot be reduced—her dispute with New Mexico cannot be settled —her surplus territory cannot be had, without her consent! This gives her a veto upon the admission of California, if coupled as proposed—gives her four vetoes! for there are four points at which her consent would be necessary, and the withholding of which upon any one point would be a veto upon the admission of California. In fact it would give her still more vetoes. For the subjects coupled together, and acted upon as a whole, must all stand or fall together; so that the veto of Texas upon any part of her own subject would be the veto of the whole with which they were coupled.

The Texas questions ought to be settled—ought to have been before she was admitted into the Union, and I proposed it then, five years ago, and have proposed it again at the present session. My proposition, heretofore, printed by order of the Senate, contains my sentiments. I am ready to vote for them; or for better, if offered; but always as a separate and substantive measure.

3. Fugitive slave bill. This is a case of run-away negroes, and in which California has no concern. She will have no slaves to run away, and none can run to her. She is too far off for that. She has no interest in the subject, and it is a degradation to her to have the question of her admission mixed up with it. In her name I protest against this dishonor, against this disgrace of having the high question of her admission thrown into *hotch-*

potch with a fugacious bill for the capture of runaway negroes.

We have a bill now—an independent one—for the recovery of these slaves. It is one of the oldest on the calendar, and warmly pressed at the commencement of the session. It must be about ripe for decision by this time. I am ready to vote upon it, and to vote anything, under the Constitution, which will be efficient and satisfactory. It is the only point, in my opinion, at which any of the non-slaveholding States, as States, have given just cause of complaint to the slaveholding States. I leave out individuals and societies, and speak of States, in their corporate capacity; and say, this affair of the runaway slaves is the only case in which any of the non-slaveholding States, in my opinion, have given just cause of complaint to slaveholding sisters. But how is it here, in this body, the appropriate one to apply the legal remedy? Any refusal on the part of northern members to legislate the remedy? We have heard many of them declare their opinions; and I see no line of East and West, dividing North from South, in these opinions. I see no geographical boundary dividing northern and southern opinions. I see no diversity of opinion but such as occurs in ordinary measures before Congress. For one, I am ready to vote at once for the passage of a fugitive slave recovery bill; but it must be as a separate and independent measure.

4. Suppression of the slave trade in the District of Columbia. This again is a subject in which California has no concern, and with which she should not be mixed. It is a subject of low degree, and not fit to be put into the balance against the admission of a State. It is a thing right in itself, and to be done by itself; and I see no reason why it is not done.

The opinion of this chamber seems to be unanimous; then why not act? I have been here thirty years, and have seen no state of parties in which this revolting traffic might not have been suppressed.

5. Abolition of slavery in the District of Columbia. I object to mixing this question with California, or with anything else, or taking it singly. I will send it to no committee. I will not even consider it. I will do as I have done for thirty years—let it alone. I will do as Congress has done for sixty years—let it alone. I will do, as I believe this Congress will do—let it alone. I will give no committee power to act upon it, either by special authorization, or by general words large enough to cover it.

6. Abolition of slavery in the forts and arsenals, navy-yards, and dockyards of the United States. I make the same objection to mixing this subject with California, or with anything else. I eschew it in *toto*, and will vote to give no committee any sort of jurisdiction over it.

7. Abolition of the slave trade between the States. Still the same answer. I will mix it with nothing, nor take it by itself. Congress has shown no disposition to meddle with it, and has no power to do so. The clause quoted by some—no one in Congress that I ever heard of—the clause to regulate commerce between the States, gives no such power; and if it did, would be precisely the contrary of what has been claimed. To "regulate" is not to destroy, but to guide and direct—to conduct with order and method, for the better success of the thing regulated. It is to protect and to promote commerce among the States that Congress is authorized to regulate it between them; and, in that sense, it is probable that Congress will have no applications to regulate the sale of slaves

between the States, nor have any disposition to do it of its own accord.

8. Abolition of slavery in the States. This again is a subject which I would not touch. The slave States are much agitated about it; but without reason, and against reason. Congress has done nothing to alarm them, and much to quiet them. Disclaimer of power—disclaimer of desire; sixty years refusal to touch it, is the highest evidence which Congress can give of its determination to abide the Constitution and its duty. This ought to be satisfactory to all slaveholders. If any one is not satisfied with this test, let him try another; let him go to the market— that quick and truthful reporter of all danger to property; and he will quickly find, from the price that is offered him, that nobody is afraid of abolition but himself.

No, sir! These four last named subjects—abolition of slavery in this District—its abolition in the forts and arsenals, dock-yards and navy-yards—its abolition in the States—and the suppression of the slave trade between the States—all belong to a class of subjects not to be touched—which Congress never has touched, and has no disposition now to touch. They are subjects which require no additional guaranties from congressional compromises. The Constitution is the compromise. It is the binding compromise, and has been faithfully kept by every Congress from 1789 to 1850; and there is no reason to suppose it will not continue to be kept. If it shall not be kept, it will be time enough, after the breach is committed, to think of the remedy—the remedy of disunion. We should no more look ahead for causes of disunion, than we should look ahead for causes of separation from our wives, or for the murder of our mothers.

*   *   *

I am for open and independent voting upon every point, and against any concoction of a committee. I am against letting it be supposed, either at home or in Europe, that the preservation of this Union depends upon the consultation of political doctors over the sick body of the Republic. Its preservation is not there—nor here—in a committee room, nor in this Chamber, nor in the hands of politicians; but in the hearts of the people, who are at home attending to their own affairs, and who will attend to the public affairs also when necessary; and who know that they themselves have enjoyed, and are enjoying, more blessings under this UNION than ever fell to the lot of man upon earth; and who are determined that their children shall have the same right to the blessings of civil and religious liberty, and the same equal chance for the wealth and honors of the country which they themselves have had. There is where the salvation of the Union lies, and not in the contrivances of politicians, or the incubations of committees.

Senator Clay's Reply

MR. President, although far from being well, suffering still under the common malady of the times—the influenza, I suppose—I feel myself called upon to make some reply to a portion of the arguments which we have just heard from the Senator from Missouri. Sir, I have to express an unfeigned regret that it is not my fortune to concur in opinion with that Senator in reference to the

mode of accomplishing a common object which we both have very much at
heart. My respect for the ability, and my
deference to the long service and great
experience of that Senator, and my
knowledge of the deep interest which he
takes, and in which I most heartily share,
in the admission of this new State as
soon as practicable, renders it extremely
unpleasant, and as I think unfortunate,
that we should differ as to the means of
accomplishing a common object.

Mr. President, I stated on Friday last,
and I have on various occasions stated,
that, for one, I was ready to vote for the
admission of California separately, by itself and unconnected with any other
measures, or in conjunction with other
measures. And I stated on that occasion
to the Senate and to the Senator from
Missouri, that I believed, as I yet believe,
that the most speedy mode of accomplishing the object which both he and I
have in view, is by combining some of
these measures in connection with California, and by this combined bill presenting subjects, which I shall presently
show are fairly connected in their nature, to the consideration of Congress at
one and the same time. The whole question between the Senator from Missouri and myself, is which is the best
mode of accomplishing the object. I say
connect the several measures together;
he says no, take California separately
and alone. Sir, I should be glad if the
experiment could be made without in-
jury to the public, that the two modes
should be tested by experience, and it
would then be ascertained whether the
Senator from Missouri or myself was correct. He has made an allusion to a remark of mine on Friday last, with reference to the difficulties that may arise on
the passage of a bill alone for the ad-

mission of California, and he has inquired what I had in contemplation at
the time I made that remark. Mr. President, I had various matters in contemplation at that time, and one was this.
About California we all know there is no
difficulty as to her admission, either separately or conjointly with other measures:
We all know perfectly well that there
are large majorities in both Houses in
favor of the admission of California. We
know at the same time that there are
great difficulties with reference to the
passage of territorial governments unconnected with the Wilmot proviso. We
know that one portion of Congress desire
very much the admission of California,
when many members comprising that
portion are opposed—some to the establishment of any governments at all for
the territories, and many of them to the
establishment of such governments without the introduction of the proviso.
Thus, whilst that party, anxious for the
accomplishment of its own views and
the satisfaction of its own wants, are
pressing on for the passage of a bill for
the separate admission of California,
they are holding back in reference to
other subjects equally important in the
great object which I trust animates the
breasts of all—the great object of quiet
and pacific action to the country. And,
besides, there are those who desire the
establishment of governments for the
territories without the proviso, but who
are willing to take the admission of California in combination with governments
for the territories without the proviso. I
did allude to other considerations, not
likely to happen in this House, but which
have happened, and may again happen
in the other house of Congress; I did
allude to what we heard said, not in approbation—far from it—but with most

decided disapprobation of it on my part. I did hear—as we know has occurred once at least on one day during this session—that if it was attempted to force on the minority of that House a measure which is unacceptable to it, and abhorrent to its feelings, without its association with other objects in view, that minority would resort, in resistance of it, not I trust to acts of violence, but to those parliamentary rules and modes of proceeding of which we have had before instances in this country, and which I myself witnessed forty years ago, in a most remarkable degree, in the House of Representatives, and which we know some consider lawful at any time to be employed. For myself, I differ perhaps from most members of this body, or of any deliberative body, on this subject. I am for the trial of mind against mind, of argument against argument, of reason against reason, and when, after such employment of our intellectual faculties, I find myself in the minority, I am for submitting to the act of the majority. I am not for resorting to adjournments, calls for the yeas and nays, and other dilatory proceedings, in order to delay that which, if the Constitution has full and fair operation, must inevitably take place. There is great loss of sleep, with great physical discomfort, in the one mode of proceeding, without any in the other. But, whilst this is my judgment, of what is proper, in deliberative bodies, other gentlemen entertain different opinions. They think it fair to employ all the parliamentary means that are vested in them by the Constitution, or by the rules which regulate the body to which they belong, to defeat, impede, or delay to any extent, the passage of the measure which they consider odious. I repeat, sir, I do not justify such a course; but we

must take man as he is, with all his weaknesses and infirmities, and we can never expect to make him as we could wish him to be.

Now, the Senator from Missouri, has chosen to characterize this measure with unfairness of proceeding. Sir, if I were disposed to retort, which I am far from doing, I could say that there had been some unfairness in the argument of the Senator from Missouri, when he endeavored to show that the pending proposition was to combine California, the territorial governments for the two proposed territories, the fixation of the line of Texas, the fugitive slave bill, the bill for abolishing the slave-trade in this District, abolition, and God Almighty knows how many other subjects, which his imagination depicted as contemplated to be introduced into our omnibus bill, and to be considered in that way. The Senator from Missouri knows perfectly well that no such purpose existed, and he has no right to infer any purpose of the kind. No longer ago than Friday last, when I misunderstood my colleague, and supposed that his object was to combine this fugitive slave bill with these measures, he rose at once and disclaimed any such intention. Sir, nobody has gone further in this proposed combination of subjects than the admission of California, the establishment of territorial governments, and—doubting its propriety, as I did on Friday, not being absolutely determined in my own mind—adding to these two measures the establishment of a suitable boundary for Texas, with the offer of an equivalent for the surrender of any title which she might be supposed to have in the territory so surrendered. Let us look, whilst on this subject of Texas, to another part of the Senator's argument, and I put it to the candor of the Senator to admit how unfair, how improper, at least, it is to suppose that, by such a combination as I have indicated, the result would be to give Texas a veto on California? Who imagines that? You pass a bill with the separate section for the admission of California, other sections in the same bill establishing governments in the two Territories, and other sections in relation to the proposition to Texas for the settlement of her boundary, making her certain offers, and this latter proposition dependent on the consent which Texas might or might not give. But suppose Texas does not give her consent, does anybody say that the other parts of the bill would become dead or nugatory? Each portion of the bill is of force and effect according to the object in view, and each might stand, although the other portion of the bill might be rendered null, in consequence of the nonconcurrence of Texas in any other power.

It has been said that it is wrong to make those who might be in favor of the admission of California, and against the establishment of territorial governments, or *vice versa*, vote on such a combination—that it would be wrong to combine them in one bill, because they would have to vote against both, not liking a portion of the bill, or for both, still disliking a portion of the bill. And we are told that what the wisdom of California suggested in her constitution—that is to say, the keeping of subjects separate and distinct—is thereby to be disregarded. Now there is very little of practicability in this idea of a total separation of subjects. Suppose you have the California bill alone before you, is that a single idea? There is first the admission of the State, and secondly the proper boundaries of the State. Now there may be Senators, if you had this single bill before you, who would say we are willing

to admit a State, to be carved out of this territory, but we are against the boundaries proposed, and why not separate it into two bills, one for the admission of the State, and the other for the fixation of its limits. Why, thus you might go on, cutting subjects up into as many parts as they are capable of being divided into, and say that each one of them shall contain a single, and only a single, idea. Take the tariff bill. It contains five hundred items usually, and we have never passed a tariff bill, or given a vote upon it, without some parts of it being objectionable to some, or that did not contain items for which some man voted against his judgment, but which he did vote for, because of other items in the same bill. And so with the course we propose. If we combine together a bill for the admission of California, and for governments for the territories, in the first place those who opposed the combination may oppose it. If it is introduced already in the bill, it may be proposed to strike out what relates to the territories; or if it is proposed that they shall be added to the bill for the admission of California, they can move amendments, call for the yeas and nays, and thus show their opposition to the association of the measures together. But suppose the majority overrules them. Suppose there is a majority in favor of the association of the measures, and then the final question is put: Will you vote for or against the bill? And what are you to do in a case of that kind? Exactly what we would do in all human concerns. There is bad and good mixed together. You may vote against it if you please in toto, because of the bad there is in it, or you may vote for it, because you approve of the greater amount of good there is in it. The question for the time is, whether there is more of the good than of the bad in the bill; and if the good outweighs the bad, that will be a further consideration for voting for the whole measure.

* * *

Mr. President, I hope I am doing a less imprudent thing in the attempt I am making to keep these subjects together, than I am doing in regard to my personal condition in occupying so much of your time. If I had supposed otherwise, I should not have said a word. But, sir, I hope I have said enough to show, first, that California would be more speedily admitted by being connected with the territories in a common bill than if it should stand separated from them: secondly, that there is no incongruity in the association of the subjects; and, thirdly, that according to precedent and all the analogies to be drawn from precedents not exactly like, but somewhat similar to, the present case, there is no impediment in the way of the course which I have proposed. And if I am right in this view, I am sure no difficulty need be apprehended. Every member of this body is desirous of restoring once more peace, harmony, and fraternal affection to this distracted people. Various projects have been suggested to accomplish that patriotic object. Amongst them a proposition has been made by the Senator from Mississippi to refer all the subjects to one committee, to be appointed by the Senate, with power to report as that committee may, upon consideration, deem it best, either a separate or a conjoint measure. The purpose of the committee is to settle, if they can, the causes of difference which exist in the country by some proposition of compromise. There are, no doubt, many men who are very wise in their own estimation, who will reject all propositions of compromise, but that is no reason why a compromise should

not be attempted to be made. I go for honorable compromise whenever it can be made. Life itself is but a compromise between death and life, the struggle continuing throughout our whole existence, until the Great Destroyer finally triumphs. All legislation, all government, all society, is formed upon the principle of mutual concession, politeness, comity, courtesy; upon these, everything is based. I bow to you to-day because you bow to me. You are respectful to me because I am respectful to you. Compromise is peculiarly appropriate among the members of a republic, as of one common family. Compromises have this recommendation, that if you concede anything, you have something conceded to you in return. Treaties are compromises made with foreign Powers contrary to what is done in a case like this. Here, if you concede anything, it is to your own brethren, to your own family. Let him who elevates himself above humanity, above its weaknesses, its infirmities, its wants, its necessities, say, if he pleases, I never will compromise, but let no one who is not above the frailties of our common nature disdain compromises.

Well, what does the honorable Senator from Mississippi propose? Here is a proposition to refer all the subjects to a committee with a view to a compromise. The honorable Senator from Missouri rises up and says no; here is one subject that you must not refer to the committee; another Senator may rise up and say here is another subject that you must not refer; and a third may rise up and say here is a third subject that you must not refer to the committee. This proposition establishes a committee the object of which is to compromise all the differences that arise out of the subject of slavery. Constitute your committee for such a purpose, and then take from them the consideration of one branch of the subject. Would this be right, sir? Can you not trust your committee? Whatever is done by the committee has to be brought before the Senate for its consideration, for confirmation or rejection at the pleasure of the Senate. If they report an improper bill, either as a separate measure, or a connected measure,

you have the controlling power. Will you not allow the subject to be considered, examined, determined upon by the committee, according to the best judgment of those to whom you confide the great and responsible duty? Sir, I am done; I ought not to have said so much, and I beg pardon of the Senate for occupying so much of their time.

SENATOR CALHOUN'S PROPOSAL TO RESTORE
A SECTIONAL EQUILIBRIUM

I HAVE, Senators, believed from the first that the agitation of the subject of slavery would, if not prevented by some timely and effective measure, end in disunion. Entertaining this opinion, I have, on all proper occasions, endeavored to call the attention of each of the two great parties which divide the country to adopt some measure to prevent so great a disaster, but without success. The agitation has been permitted to proceed, with almost no attempt to resist it, until it has reached a period when it can no longer be disguised or denied that the Union is in danger. You have thus had forced upon you the greatest and the gravest question that can ever come under your consideration: How can the Union be preserved?

To give a satisfactory answer to this mighty question, it is indispensable to have an accurate and thorough knowledge of the nature and the character of the cause by which the Union is endangered. Without such knowledge it is impossible to pronounce, with any certainty, by what measure it can be saved; just as it would be impossible for a physician to pronounce, in the case of some dangerous disease, with any certainty,

by what remedy the patient could be saved, without familiar knowledge of the nature and character of the cause of the disease. The first question, then, presented for consideration, in the investigation I propose to make, in order to obtain such knowledge, is: What is it that has endangered the Union?

To this question there can be but one answer: that the immediate cause is the almost universal discontent which pervades all the States composing the southern section of the Union. This widely extended discontent is not of recent origin. It commenced with the agitation of the slavery question, and has been increasing ever since. The next question, going one step further back, is: What has caused this widely diffused and almost universal discontent?

It is a great mistake to suppose, as is by some, that it originated with demagogues, who excited the discontent with the intention of aiding their personal advancement, or with the disappointed ambition of certain politicians, who resorted to it as the means of retrieving their fortunes. On the contrary, all the great political influences of the section were arrayed against excitement, and exerted to the utmost to keep the people quiet. The great mass of the people of the South were divided, as in the other section, into Whigs and Democrats. The leaders and the presses of both parties in the South were very solicitous to prevent excitement and to preserve quiet; because it was seen that the effects of the former would necessarily tend to weaken, if not destroy, the political ties which united them with their respective parties in the other section. Those who know the strength of party ties will readily appreciate the immense force which this cause exerted against agitation and in favor of preserving quiet. But, as great as it was, it was not sufficiently so to prevent the wide-spread discontent which now pervades the section. No; some cause, far deeper and more powerful than the one supposed, must exist, to account for discontent so wide and deep. The question, then, recurs: What is the cause of this discontent? It will be found in the belief of the people of the southern States, as prevalent as the discontent itself, that they cannot remain, as things now are, consistently with honor and safety, in the Union. The next question to be considered is: What has caused this belief?

One of the causes is, undoubtedly, to be traced to the long-continued agitation of the slave question on the part of the North, and the many aggressions which they have made on the rights of the South during the time. I will not enumerate them at present, as it will be done hereafter, in its proper place.

There is another, lying back of it, with which this is intimately connected, that may be regarded as the great and primary cause. That is to be found in the fact that the equilibrium between the two sections in the Government, as it stood when the constitution was ratified and the Government put in action, has been destroyed. At that time there was nearly a perfect equilibrium between the two, which afforded ample means to each to protect itself against the aggression of the other; but, as it now stands, one section has the exclusive power of controlling the Government, which leaves the other without any adequate means of protecting itself against its encroachment and oppression. To place this subject distinctly before you, I have, Senators, prepared a brief statistical statement, showing the relative weight of the two sections in the Government under the first census of 1790 and the last census of 1840.

According to the former, the population of the United States, including Vermont, Kentucky, and Tennessee, which then were in their incipient condition of becoming States, but were not actually admitted, amounted to 3,929,827. Of this number the northern States had 1,977,899, and the southern 1,952,072, making a difference of only 25,827 in favor of the former States. The number of States, including Vermont, Kentucky, and Tennessee, was sixteen; of which eight, including Vermont, belonged to the northern section, and eight, including Kentucky and Tennessee, to the southern; making an equal division of the States between the two sections under the first census. There was a small preponderance in the House of Representatives, and in the electoral college, in favor of the northern, owing to the fact, that, according to the provisions of the Constitution, in estimating Federal numbers, five slaves count but three; but it was too small to affect sensibly the perfect equilibrium which, with that exception, existed at the time. Such was the equality of the two sections when the States composing them agreed to enter into a Federal Union. Since then the equilibrium between them has been greatly disturbed.

According to the last census the aggregate population of the United States amounted to 17,063,357, of which the northern section contained 9,728,920 and the southern 7,334,437, making a difference, in round numbers, of 2,400,000. The number of States had increased from sixteen to twenty-six, making an addition of ten States. In the meantime the position of Delaware had become doubtful as to which section she properly belongs. Considering her as neutral, the northern States will have thirteen and the southern States twelve; making a difference in the Senate of two Senators in favor of the former. According to the apportionment under the census of 1840, there were 223 members of the House of Representatives, of which the northern States had 135 and the southern States (considering Delaware as neutral) 87; making a difference in favor of the former in the House of Representatives of 48. The difference in the Senate of two members, added to this, gives to the North in the electoral college a majority of 50. Since the census of 1840 four States have been added to the Union; Iowa, Wisconsin, Florida, and Texas. They leave the difference in the Senate as it stood when the census was taken; but add two to the side of the North in the House, making the present majority in the House in its favor 50, and in the electoral college 52.

The result of the whole is to give the northern section a predominance in every part of the Government, and thereby concentrate in it the two elements which constitute the Federal Government—a majority of States and a majority of their population, estimated in federal numbers. Whatever section concentrates the

two in itself possesses the control of the entire Government.

But we are just at the close of the sixth decade, and the commencement of the seventh. The census is to be taken this year, which must add greatly to the decided preponderance of the North in the House of Representatives and in the electoral college. The prospect is, also, that a great increase will be added to its present preponderance in the Senate during the period of the decade, by the addition of new States. Two Territories, Oregon and Minnesota, are already in progress, and strenuous efforts are making to bring in three additional States from the territory recently conquered from Mexico; which, if successful, will add three other States in a short time to the northern section, making five States; and increasing the present number of its States from fifteen to twenty, and of its Senators from thirty to forty. On the contrary, there is not a single territory in progress in the southern section, and no certainty that any additional State will be added to it during the decade. The prospect then, is, that the two sections in the Senate, should the efforts now made to exclude the South from the newly acquired territories succeed, will stand, before the end of the decade, twenty northern States to twelve southern (considering Delaware as neutral), and forty northern Senators to twenty-four southern. This great increase of Senators, added to the great increase of members of the House of Representatives and the electoral college on the part of the North, which must take place under the next decade, will effectually and irretrievably destroy the equilibrium which existed when the Government commenced.

Had this destruction been the operation of time, without the interference of

Government, the South would have had no reason to complain; but such was not the fact. It was caused by the legislation of this Government, which was appointed as the common agent of all, and charged with the protection of the interests and security of all. The legislation by which it has been effected may be classed under three heads. The first is, that series of acts by which the South has been excluded from the common territory belonging to all of the States, as the members of the Federal Union, and which have had the effect of extending vastly the portion allotted to the Northern section, and restricting within narrow limits the portion left the South; the next consists in adopting a system of revenue and disbursements, by which an undue proportion of the burden of taxation has been imposed upon the South, and an undue proportion of its proceeds appropriated to the North; and the last is a system of political measures by which the original character of the Government has been radically changed. I propose to bestow upon each of these, in the order they stand, a few remarks, with the view of showing that it is owing to the action of this Government that the equilibrium between the two sections has been destroyed, and the whole powers of the system centered in a sectional majority.

The first of the series of acts by which the South was deprived of its due share of the territories, originated with the Confederacy, which preceded the existence of this Government. It is to be found in the provision of the ordinance of 1787. Its effect was to exclude the South entirely from that vast and fertile region which lies between the Ohio and the Mississippi rivers, now embracing five States and one Territory. The next of the series is the Missouri compromise, which excluded the South from that large portion of Louisiana which lies north of 36° 30', excepting what is included in the State of Missouri. The last of the series excluded the South from the whole of the Oregon Territory. All these, in the slang of the day, were what are called slave territories, and not free soil; that is, territories belonging to slaveholding powers, and open to the emigration of masters with their slaves. By these several acts, the South was excluded from 1,238,025 square miles, an extent of country considerably exceeding the entire valley of the Mississippi. To the South was left the portion of the Territory of Louisiana lying south of 36° 30', and the portion north of it included in the State of Missouri; the portion lying south of 36° 30', including the States of Louisiana and Arkansas; and the territory lying west of the latter and south of 36° 30', called the Indian country. These, with the Territory of Florida, now the State, makes in the whole 283,-503 square miles. To this must be added the territory acquired with Texas. If the whole should be added to the southern section, it would make an increase of 325,520, which would make the whole left to the South 609,023. But a large part of Texas is still in contest between the two sections, which leaves it uncertain what will be the real extent of the portion of territory that may be left to the South.

I have not included the territory recently acquired by the treaty with Mexico. The North is making the most strenuous efforts to appropriate the whole to herself, by excluding the South from every foot of it. If she should succeed, it will add to that from which the South has already been excluded 526,078 square miles, and would increase the whole which the North has appropriated to herself to 1,764,023, not including the portion that she may succeed in excluding us from in Texas. To sum up the whole, the United States, since they declared their independence, have acquired 2,373,046 square miles of territory, from which the North will have excluded the South, if she should succeed in monopolizing the newly acquired territories, from about three-fourths of the whole, leaving to the South but about one-fourth.

Such is the first and great cause that has destroyed the equilibrium between the two sections in the Government.

*   *   *

But while these measures were destroying the equilibrium between the two sections, the action of the Government was leading to a radical change in its character, by concentrating all the power of the system in itself. The occasion will not permit me to trace the measures by which this great change has been consummated. If it did, it would not be difficult to show that the process commenced at an early period of the Government; that it proceeded, almost without interruption, step by step, until it absorbed virtually its entire powers. But, without going through the whole process to establish the fact, it may be done satisfactorily by a very short statement.

That the Government claims, and practically maintains, the right to decide in the last resort as to the extent of its powers, will scarcely be denied by anyone conversant with the political history of the country. That it also claims the right to resort to force to maintain whatever power she claims, against all opposition, is equally certain. Indeed it is apparent, from what we daily hear, that this has become the prevailing and fixed opinion of a great majority of the community. Now, I ask, what limitation can possibly be placed upon the powers of a Government claiming and exercising such rights? And, if none can be, how can the separate governments of the States maintain and protect the powers reserved to them by the Constitution, or the people of the several States maintain those which are reserved to them, and among others, the sovereign powers by which they ordained and established, not only their separate State constitutions and governments, but also the Constitution and Government of the United States? But, if they have no constitutional means of maintaining them against the right claimed by this Government, it necessarily follows that they hold them at its pleasure and discretion, and that all the powers of the system are in reality concentrated in it. It also follows that the character of the Government has been changed, in consequence, from a Federal Republic, as it originally came from the hands of its framers, and that it has been changed into a great national consolidated Democracy. It has indeed, at present, all the characteristics of the latter, and not one of the former, although it still retains its outward form.

The result of the whole of these causes combined is, that the North has acquired a decided ascendancy over every department of this Government, and through it a control over all the powers of the system. A single section, governed by the will of the numerical majority, has now, in fact, the control of the Government and the entire powers of the system. What was once a constitutional Federal Republic is now converted, in reality, into one as absolute as that of the Autocrat of Russia, and as despotic in its tendency as any absolute Government that ever existed.

As, then, the North has the absolute control over the Government, it is manifest that on all questions between it and the South, where there is a diversity of interests, the interests of the latter will be sacrificed to the former, however oppressive the effects may be, as the South possesses no means by which it can resist through the action of the Government. But if there was no question of vital importance to the South, in reference to which there was a diversity of views between the two sections, this state of things might be endured without the hazard of destruction to the South. But such is not the fact. There is a question of vital importance to the southern section, in reference to which the views and feelings of the two sections are as opposite and hostile as they can possibly be.

I refer to the relation between the two races in the southern section, which constitutes a vital portion of her social organization. Every portion of the North entertains views and feelings more or less hostile to it. Those most opposed and hostile regard it as a sin, and consider themselves under the most sacred obligation to use every effort to destroy it. Indeed to the extent that they conceive they have power, they regard themselves as implicated in the sin, and responsible for suppressing it by the use of all and every means. Those less opposed and hostile, regard it as a crime—an offence against humanity, as they call it; and although not so fanatical, feel themselves bound to use all efforts to effect the same object; while those who are least opposed and hostile, regard it as a blot and a stain on the character of what they call the nation, and feel themselves accordingly bound to give it no countenance or support. On the contrary, the southern section regards the relation as one which cannot be destroyed without subjecting the two races to the greatest calamity, and the section to poverty, desolation,

and wretchedness; and accordingly they feel bound by every consideration of interest and safety, to defend it.

This hostile feeling on the part of the North towards the social organization of the South long lay dormant, but it only required some cause to act on those who felt most intensely that they were responsible for its continuance, to call it into action. The increasing power of this Government, and of the control of the northern section over all its departments, furnished the cause. It was this which made an impression on the minds of many that there was little or no restraint to prevent the Government from doing whatever it might choose to do. This was sufficient of itself to put the most fanatical portion of the North in action for the purpose of destroying the existing relation between the two races in the South.

*　*　*

It is a great mistake to suppose that disunion can be effected by a single blow. The cords which bind these States together in one common Union are far too numerous and powerful for that. Disunion must be the work of time. It is only through a long process, and successively, that the cords can be snapped, until the whole fabric falls asunder. Already the agitation of the slavery question has snapped some of the most important, and has greatly weakened all the others, as I shall proceed to show.

The cords that bind the States together are not only many, but various in character. Some are spiritual or ecclesiastical; some political; others social. Some appertain to the benefit conferred by the Union, and others to the feeling of duty and obligation.

The strongest of those of a spiritual and ecclesiastical nature consisted in the unity of the great religious denominations, all of which originally embraced the whole Union. All these denominations, with the exception, perhaps, of the Catholics, were organized very much upon the principle of our political institutions; beginning with smaller meetings corresponding with the political divisions of the country, their organization terminated in one great central assemblage, corresponding very much with the character of Congress. At these meetings the principal clergymen and lay members of the respective denominations from all parts of the Union met to transact business relating to their common concerns. It was not confined to what appertained to the doctrines and discipline of the respective denominations, but extended to plans for disseminating the Bible, establishing missionaries, distributing tracts, and of establishing presses for the publication of tracts, newspapers, and periodicals, with a view of diffusing religious information, and for the support of the doctrines and creeds of the denomination. All this combined, contributed greatly to strengthen the bonds of the Union. The strong ties which held each denomination together formed a strong cord to hold the whole Union together; but, as powerful as they were, they have not been able to resist the explosive effect of slavery agitation.

The first of these cords which snapped, under its explosive force, was that of the powerful Methodist Episcopal Church. The numerous and strong ties which held it together are all broke, and its unity gone. They now form separate churches, and, instead of that feeling of attachment and devotion to the interests of the whole church which was formerly felt, they are now arrayed into two hostile bodies, engaged in litigation about what was formerly their common property.

The next cord that snapped was that of the Baptists, one of the largest and most respectable of the denominations. That of the Presbyterian is not entirely snapped, but some of its strands have given away. That of the Episcopal Church is the only one of the four great Protestant denominations which remains unbroken and entire.

The strongest cord of a political character consists of the many and strong ties that have held together the two great parties, which have, with some modifications, existed from the beginning of the Government. They both extended to every portion of the Union, and strongly contributed to hold all its parts together. But this powerful cord has fared no better than the spiritual. It resisted for a long time the explosive tendency of the agitation, but has finally snapped under its force—if not entirely, in a great measure. Nor is there one of the remaining cords which have not been greatly weakened. To this extent the Union has already been destroyed by agitation, in the only way it can be, by snapping asunder and weakening the cords which bind it together.

If the agitation goes on, the same force, acting with increased intensity, as has been shown, will finally snap every cord, when nothing will be left to hold the States together except force. But surely that can, with no propriety of language, be called a union, when the only means by which the weaker is held connected with the stronger portion is *force.* It may, indeed, keep them connected; but the connection will partake much more of the character of subjugation, on the part of the weaker to the stronger, than the union of free, independent, and sovereign States, in one confederation, as they stood in the early stages of the Government, and which only is worthy of the sacred name of union.

Having now, Senators, explained what it is that endangers the Union, and traced it to its cause, and explained its nature and character, the question again recurs, How can the Union be saved? To this I answer, there is but one way by which it can be, and that is, by adopting such measures as will satisfy the States belonging to the southern section that they can remain in the Union consistently with their honor and their safety. There is, again, only one way by which that can be effected, and that is, by removing the causes by which this belief has been produced. Do *that,* and discontent will cease, harmony and kind feelings between the sections be restored, and every apprehension of danger to the Union removed. The question then is, By what can this be done? But, before I undertake to answer this question, I propose to show by what the Union cannot be saved.

It cannot, then, be saved by eulogies on the Union, however splendid or numerous. The cry of "Union, Union, the glorious Union!" can no more prevent disunion than the cry of "Health, health, glorious health!" on the part of the physician can save a patient lying dangerously ill. So long as the Union, instead of being regarded as a protector, is regarded in the opposite character, by not much less than a majority of the States, it will be in vain to attempt to conciliate them by pronouncing eulogies on it.

*   *   *

How can the Union be saved? There is but one way by which it can with any certainty; and that is, by a full and final settlement, on the principle of justice, of all the questions at issue between the two sections. The South asks for justice, simple justice, and less she ought not to take. She has no compromise to offer but the Constitution, and no concession or surrender to make. She has already surrendered so much that she has little left to surrender. Such a settlement would go to the root of the evil, and remove all cause of discontent, by satisfying the South she could remain honorably and safely in the Union, and thereby restore the harmony and fraternal feelings between the sections which existed anterior to the Missouri agitation. Nothing else can, with any certainty, finally and forever settle the questions at issue, terminate agitation, and save the Union.

But can this be done? Yes, easily; not by the weaker party, for it can of itself do nothing—not even protect itself—but by the stronger. The North has only to will it to accomplish it—to do justice by conceding to the South an equal right in the acquired territory, and to do her duty by causing the stipulations relative to fugitive slaves to be faithfully fulfilled—to cease the agitation of the slave question, and to provide for the insertion of a provision in the Constitution, by an amendment, which will restore to the South in substance the power she possessed of protecting herself, before the equilibrium between the sections was destroyed by the action of this Government. There will be no difficulty in devising such a provision—one that will protect the South, and which at the same time will improve and strengthen the Government, instead of impairing and weakening it.

[Editor's Note: While Calhoun did not specify the guarantees that should be given to the South in a constitutional amendment, many of his senatorial colleagues were probably aware of a specific proposal in his *Discourse on the Constitution,* published shortly after Calhoun's death on April 1, 1850. This was a proposal to create a dual executive, a President elected by each section, each with a legislative veto. Charles Wiltse is convinced, however, that Calhoun in this last speech merely intended to state the principle of equilibrium and to leave the particular devices for constitutional guarantees to the Senate. Cf. *John C. Calhoun, Sectionalist, 1840–50,* pp. 465–468].

DANIEL WEBSTER'S SEVENTH OF MARCH SPEECH

MR. President, I wish to speak to-day, not as a Massachusetts man, nor as a northern man, but as an American, and a member of the Senate of the United States. It is fortunate that there is a Senate of the United States; a body not yet moved from its propriety, not lost to a just sense of its own dignity, and its own high responsibilities, and a body to which the country looks with confidence, for wise, moderate, patriotic, and healing counsels. It is not to be denied that we live in the midst of strong agitations, and surrounded by very considerable dangers to our institutions of government. The imprisoned winds are let loose. The East, the West, the North, and the stormy South, all combine to throw the whole ocean into commotion, to toss its billows to the skies, and to disclose its profoundest depths. I do not expect, Mr. President, to hold, or to be fit to hold, the helm in combat of the political elements; but I have a duty to perform, and I mean to perform it with fidelity—not without a sense of the surrounding dangers, but not without hope. I have a part to act, not for my own security or safety, for I am looking out for no fragment upon which to float away from the wreck, if wreck there must be, but for the good of the whole, and the preservation of the whole; and there is that which will keep me to my duty during this struggle, whether the sun and the stars shall appear, or shall not appear, for many days. I speak to-day for the preservation of the Union. "Hear me for my cause." I speak to-day, out of a solicitous and anxious heart, for the restoration to the country of that quiet and

that harmony which make the blessings of this Union so rich and so dear to us all. These are the topics that I propose to myself to discuss; these are the motives, and the sole motives, that influence me in the wish to communicate my opinions to the Senate and the country; and if I can do anything, however little, for the promotion of these ends, I shall have accomplished all that I desire.

* * *

On other occasions, in debates here, I have expressed my determination to vote for no acquisition, or cession, or annexation, North or South, East or West. My opinion has been, that we have territory enough, and that we should follow the Spartan maxim, "Improve, adorn what you have, seek no farther." I think that it was in some observations that I made here on the three million loan bill, that I avowed that sentiment. In short, sir, the sentiment has been avowed quite as often, in as many places, and before as many assemblages, as any of the humble sentiments of mine ought to be avowed.

But now that, under certain conditions, Texas is in with all her territories, as a slave State, with a solemn pledge that if she is divided into many States, those States may come in as slave States south of 36° 30', how are we to deal with it? I know no way of honorable legislation, but, when the proper time comes for the enactment, to carry into effect all that we have stipulated to do. I do not entirely agree with my honorable friend from Tennessee, [Mr. Bell] that, as soon as the time comes when she is entitled to another Representative, we should

Congressional Globe, XXII, Part 1, 1st session, 31st Congress, 1849–50, from pages 476–483.

create a new State. The rule in regard to it I take to be this: that when we have created new States out of territories, we have generally gone upon the idea, that when there is population enough to form a State—sixty thousand, or some such thing—we would create a State; but it may be thought quite a different thing when a State is divided, and two or more States made out of it. It does not follow, in such a case, that the same rule of apportionment should be applied. That, however, is a matter for the consideration of Congress when the proper time arrives. I may not be here—I may have no vote to give on the occasion; but I wish it to be distinctly understood today, that according to my view of the matter, this Government is solemnly pledged, by law, to create new States out of Texas, with her consent, when her population shall justify such a proceeding, and so far as such States are formed out of Texan territory lying south of 36° 30', to let them come in as slave States. That is the meaning of the resolution which our friends, the northern Democracy, have left us to fulfill; and I, for one, mean to fulfill it, because I will not violate the faith of the Government.

Now, as to California and New Mexico, I hold slavery to be excluded from those territories by a law even superior to that which admits and sanctions it in Texas—I mean the law of nature—of physical geography—the law of the formation of the earth. That law settles forever, with a strength beyond all terms of human enactment, that slavery cannot exist in California or New Mexico. Understand me, sir—I mean slavery as we regard it; slaves in the gross, of the colored race, transferable by sale and delivery, like other property. I shall not discuss that point. I leave it to the learned gentlemen who have undertaken to discuss it; but I suppose there is no slave of that description in California now. I understand that *peonism,* a sort of penal servitude, exists there; or, rather, a voluntary sale of a man and his offspring for debt, as it is arranged and exists in some parts of California and New Mexico. But what I mean to say is, that African slavery, as we see it among us, is as utterly impossible to find itself, or to be found in Mexico, as any other natural impossibility. California and New Mexico are Asiatic in their formation and scenery. They are composed of vast ridges of mountains, of enormous height, with sometimes broken ridges and deep valleys. The sides of these mountains are barren—entirely barren—their tops capped by perennial snow. There may be in California, now made free by its constitution—and no doubt there are—some tracts of valuable land. But it is not so in New Mexico. Pray, what is the evidence which any gentleman has obtained on this subject, from information sought by himself or communicated by others? I have inquired, and read all I could, to obtain information on this subject. What is there in New Mexico that could by any possibility induce any body to go there with slaves? There are some narrow strips of tillable land on the borders of the rivers; but the rivers themselves dry up before mid-summer is gone. All that the people can do is to raise some little articles—some little wheat for their tortillas—and all that by irrigation. And who expects to see a hundred black men cultivating tobacco, corn, cotton, rice, or anything else, on lands in New Mexico, made fertile only by irrigation? I look upon it, therefore, as a fixed fact, to use an expression current to the day, that both California and New Mexico are destined to be free, so far as they are settled at all, which I believe, especially in regard to New Mexico, will be very little for a great length of time—free by the arrangement of things by the Power above us. I have therefore to say, in this respect also, that this country is fixed for freedom, to as many persons as shall ever live there, by as irrepealable and a more irrepealable law, than the law that attaches to the right of holding slaves in Texas; and I will say further, that if a resolution, or a law, were now before us, to provide a territorial government for New Mexico, I would not vote to put any prohibition into it whatever. The use of such a prohibition would be idle, as it respects any effect it would have upon the territory; and I would not take pains to reaffirm an ordinance of nature, nor to re-enact the will of God. And I would put in no Wilmot proviso, for the purpose of a taunt or a reproach. I would put into it no evidence of the votes of superior power, to wound the pride, even whether a just pride, a rational pride, or an irrational pride—to wound the pride of the gentlemen who belong to the southern States. I have no such object—no such purpose. They would think it a taunt— an indignity. They would think it to be an act taking away from them what they regard a proper equality of privilege; and whether they expect to realize any benefit from it or not, they would think it a theoretic wrong—that something more or less derogatory to their character and their rights had taken place. I propose to inflict no such wound upon any body, unless something essentially important to the country, and efficient to the preservation of liberty and freedom, is to be effected. Therefore, I repeat, sir—and I repeat it because I wish it to be understood—that I do not propose to address the Senate often on this subject.

I desire to pour out all my heart in as plain a manner as possible; and I say again, that if a proposition were now here for a government for New Mexico, and it was moved to insert a provision for a prohibition of slavery, I would not vote for it.

*　　*　　*

Mr. President, in the excited times in which we live, there is found to exist a state of crimination and recrimination between the North and the South. There are lists of grievances produced by each; and those grievances, real or supposed, alienate the minds of one portion of the country from the other, exasperate the feelings, subdue the sense of fraternal connection, and patriotic love, and mutual regard. I shall bestow a little attention, sir, upon these various grievances, produced on the one side and on the other. I begin with the complaints of South; I will not answer, farther than I have, the general statements of the honorable Senator from South Carolina, that the North has grown upon the South in consequence of the manner of administering this Government, in the collecting of its revenues, and so forth. These are disputed topics, and I have no inclination to enter into them. But I will state these complaints, especially one complaint of the South, which has in my opinion just foundation; and that is, that there has been found at the North, among individuals and among the Legislatures of the North, a disinclination to perform, fully, their constitutional duties, in regard to the return of persons bound to service, who have escaped into the free States. In that respect, it is my judgment that the South is right, and the North is wrong. Every member of every northern Legislature is bound, by oath, like every other officer in the country, to support the Constitution of the United States; and this article of the Constitution, which says to these States, they shall deliver up fugitives from service, is as binding in honor and conscience as any other article. No man fulfills his duty in any Legislature who sets himself to find excuses, evasions, escapes from this constitutional obligation. I have always thought that the Constitution addressed itself to the Legislatures of the States themselves, or to the States themselves. It says, that those persons escaping to other States, shall be delivered up, and I confess I have always been of the opinion, that it was an injunction upon the States themselves. When it is said, that a person escaping into another State, and becoming therefore within the jurisdiction of that State, shall be delivered up, it seems to me the import of the passage is, that the State itself, in obedience to the Constitution, shall cause him to be delivered up. That is my judgment. I have always entertained that opinion, and I entertain it now. But when the subject, some years ago, was put before the Supreme Court of the United States, the majority of the judges held that the power, to cause fugitives from service to be delivered up, was a power to be exercised under the authority of this Government. I do not know, on the whole, that it may not have been a fortunate decision. My habit is to respect the result of judicial deliberations and the solemnity of judicial decisions. But, as it now stands, the business of seeing that these fugitives are delivered up, resides in the power of Congress, and the national judicature, and my friend at the head of the Judiciary Committee has a bill on the subject, now before the Senate, with some amendments to it, which

I propose to support, with all its provisions, to the fullest extent. And I desire to call the attention of all sober-minded men, of all conscientious men, in the North, of all men who are not carried away by any fanatical idea, or by any false idea whatever, to their constitutional obligations. I put it to all the sober and sound minds at the North, as a question of morals and a question of conscience, What right have they, in all their legislative capacity, or any other, to endeavor to get round this Constitution, to embarrass the free exercise of the rights secured by the Constitution, to the persons whose slaves escape from them? None at all—none at all. Neither in the forum of conscience, nor before the face of the Constitution, are they justified, in my opinion. Of course, it is a matter for their consideration. They probably, in the turmoil of the times, have not stopped to consider of this; they have followed what seemed to be the current of thought and of motives as the occasion arose, and neglected to investigate fully the real question, and to consider their constitutional obligations, as I am sure, if they did consider, they would fulfill them with alacrity. Therefore, I repeat, sir, that here is a ground of complaint against the North, well founded, which ought to be removed—which it is now in the power of the different departments of this Government to remove— which calls for the enactment of proper laws, authorizing the judicature of this Government, in the several States, to do all that is necessary for the recapture of fugitive slaves, and for the restoration of them to those who claim them. Wherever I go, and whenever I speak on the subject—and when I speak here, I desire to speak to the whole North—I say that the South has been injured in this respect, and has a right to complain; and the North has been too careless of what I think the Constitution peremptorily and emphatically enjoins upon it as a duty.

*   *   *

There are also complaints of the North against the South. I need not go over them particularly. The first and gravest is, that, the North adopted the Constitution, recognizing the existence of slavery in the States, and recognizing the right, to a certain extent, of representation of the slaves in Congress, under a state of sentiment and expectation which do not now exist; and that, by events, by circumstances, by the eagerness of the South to acquire territory, and extend their slave population, the North finds itself, in regard to the influence of the South and the North, of the free States and the slave States, where it never did expect to find itself when they entered the compact of the Constitution. They complain, therefore, that, instead of slavery being regarded as an evil, as it was then, an evil, which all hoped would be extinguished gradually, it is now regarded by the South as an institution to be cherished, and preserved, and extended —an institution which the South has already extended to the utmost of her power by the acquisition of new territory. Well, then, passing from that, everybody in the North reads; and everybody reads whatsoever the newspapers contain; and the newspapers, some of them—especially those presses to which I have alluded—are careful to spread about among the people every reproachful sentiment uttered by any southern man bearing at all against the North— everything that is calculated to exasperate, to alienate; and there are many such things, as everybody will admit, from the

South, or some portion of it, which are spread abroad among the reading people; and they do exasperate, and alienate, and produce a most mischievous effect upon the public mind at the North. Sir, I would not notice things of this sort appearing in obscure quarters; but one thing has occurred in this debate which struck me very forcibly. An honorable member from Louisiana addressed us the other day on this subject. I suppose there is not a more amiable and worthy gentleman in this chamber, nor a gentleman who would be more slow to give offense to anybody, and he did not mean in his remarks to give offense. But what did he say? Why, sir, he took pains to run a contrast between the slaves of the South and the laboring people of the North, giving the preference in all points of condition, and comfort, and happiness, to the slaves of the South. The honorable member doubtless did not suppose that he gave any offense, or did any injustice. He was merely expressing his opinion. But does he know how remarks of that sort will be received by the laboring people of the North? Why, who are the laboring people of the North? They are the North. They are the people who cultivate their own farms with their own hands—freeholders, educated men, independent men. Let me say, sir, that five sixths of the whole property of the North, is in the hands of the laborers of the North; they cultivate their farms, they educate their children, they provide the means of independence; if they are not freeholders, they earn wages; these wages accumulate, are turned into capital, into new freeholds; and small capitalists are created. That is the case, and such the course of things, with us, among the industrious, and frugal. And what can these people think when so respectable and worthy a gentleman as the member from Louisiana, undertakes to prove that the absolute ignorance, and the abject slavery of the South, is more in conformity with the high purposes and destinies of immortal, rational, human beings, than the educated, the independent free laborers of the North?

There is a more tangible, and irritating cause of grievance, at the North. Free blacks are constantly employed in the vessels of the North, generally as cooks or stewards. When the vessel arrives, these free colored men are taken on shore, by the police or municipal authority, imprisoned, and kept in prison, till the vessel is again ready to sail. This is not only irritating, but exceedingly inconvenient in practice, and seems altogether unjustifiable, and oppressive. Mr. Hoar's mission, some time ago, to South Carolina, was a well-intended effort to remove this cause of complaint. The North thinks such imprisonment illegal, and unconstitutional; as the cases occur constantly and frequently, they think it a great grievance.

Now, sir, so far as any of these grievances have their foundation in matters of law, they can be redressed, and ought to be redressed; and so far as they have foundation in matters of opinion, in sentiment, in mutual crimination and recrimination, all that we can do is, to endeavor to allay the agitation, and cultivate a better feeling and more fraternal sentiments between the South and the North.

Mr. President, I should much prefer to have heard, from every member on this floor, declarations of opinion that this Union should never be dissolved, than the declaration of opinion that in any case, under the pressure of any circumstances, such a dissolution was possible.

I hear with pain, and anguish, and distress, the word secession, especially when it falls from the lips of those who are eminently patriotic, and known to the country, and known all over the world, for their political services. Secession! Peaceable secession! Sir, your eyes and mine are never destined to see that miracle. The dismemberment of this vast country without convulsion! The breaking up of the fountains of the great deep without ruffling the surface! Who is so foolish—I beg everybody's pardon—as to expect to see any such thing? Sir, he who sees these States, now revolving in harmony around a common centre, and expects to see them quit their places and fly off without convulsion, may look the next hour to see the heavenly bodies rush from their spheres, and jostle against each other in the realms of space, without producing the crush of the universe. There can be no such thing as a peaceable secession. Peaceable secession is an utter impossibility. Is the great Constitution under which we live here—covering this whole country—is it to be thawed and melted away by secession, as the snows on the mountain melt under the influence of a vernal sun—disappear almost unobserved, and die off? No, sir! no, sir! I will not state what might produce the disruption of the States; but, sir, I see it as plainly as I see the sun in heaven—I see that disruption must produce such a war as I will not describe, in its twofold characters.

Peaceable secession! peaceable secession! The concurrent agreement of all the members of this great Republic to separate! A voluntary separation, with alimony on one side and on the other. Why, what would be the result? Where is the line to be drawn? What States are to secede? What is to remain American?

What am I to be?—an American no longer? Where is the flag of the Republic to
remain? Where is the eagle still to tow-
er? or is he to cower, and shrink, and
fall to the ground? Why, sir, our ancestors—our fathers, and our grandfathers,
those of them that are yet living among
us with prolonged lives—would rebuke
and reproach us; and our children, and
our grandchildren, would cry out, Shame
upon us! if we, of this generation, should
dishonor these ensigns of the power of
the Government, and the harmony of the
Union, which is every day felt among us
with so much joy and gratitude. What is
to become of the army? What is to become of the navy? What is to become of
the public lands? How is each of the
thirty States to defend itself? I know, although the idea has not been stated distinctly, there is to be a southern Confederacy. I do not mean, when I allude
to this statement, that any one seriously
contemplates such a state of things. I do
not mean to say that it is true, but I have
heard it suggested elsewhere, that that
idea has originated in a design to separate. I am sorry, sir, that it has ever been
thought of, talked of, or dreamed of, in
the wildest flights of human imagination.
But the idea must be of a separation, including the slave States upon one side,
and the free States on the other. Sir,
there is not—I may express myself too
strongly perhaps—but some things, some
moral things, are almost as impossible,
as other natural or physical things; and
I hold the idea of a separation of these
States—those that are free to form one
government, and those that are slaveholding to form another—as a moral impossibility. We could not separate the
States by any such line, if we were to
draw it. We could not sit down here to-
day, and draw a line of separation, that
would satisfy any five men in the coun-

try. There are natural causes that would
keep and tie us together, and there are
social and domestic relations which we
could not break, if we would, and which
we should not, if we could. Sir, nobody
can look over the face of this country at
the present moment—nobody can see
where its population is the most dense
and growing—without being ready to admit, and compelled to admit, that, ere
long, America will be in the valley of the
Mississippi.

Well, now, sir, I beg to inquire what
the wildest enthusiast has to say, on the
possibility of cutting off that river, and
leaving free States at its source and its
branches, and slave States down near
its mouth? Pray, sir—pray, sir, let me say
to the people of this country, that these
things are worthy of their pondering and
of their consideration. Here, sir, are five
millions of freemen in the free States
north of the river Ohio; can anybody suppose that this population can be severed
by a line that divides them from the territory of a foreign and an alien government, down somewhere, the Lord knows
where, upon the lower banks of the Mississippi? What will become of Missouri?
Will she join the arrondissement of the
slave States? Shall the man from the
Yellow Stone and the Platte be connected in the new Republic with the man
who lives on the southern extremity of
the Cape of Florida? Sir, I am ashamed
to pursue this line of remark. I dislike
it—I have an utter disgust for it. I would
rather hear of natural blasts and mil-
dews, war, pestilence, and famine, than
to hear gentlemen talk of secession. To
break up! to break up this great Government! to dismember this great country! to astonish Europe with an act of
folly, such as Europe for two centuries
has never beheld in any government! No,
sir! no, sir! There will be no secession.

Gentlemen are not serious when they talk of secession.

*   *   *

And now, Mr. President, instead of speaking of the possibility or utility of secession, instead of dwelling in these caverns of darkness, instead of groping with those ideas so full of all that is horrid and horrible, let us come out into the light of day; let us enjoy the fresh air of liberty and union: let us cherish those hopes which belong to us; let us devote ourselves to those great objects that are fit for our consideration and our action; let us raise our conceptions to the magnitude and the importance of the duties that devolve upon us; let our comprehension be as broad as the country for which we act, our aspirations as high as its certain destiny; let us not be pigmies in a case that calls for men. Never did there devolve, on any generation of men, higher trusts than now devolve upon us for the preservation of this Constitution, and the harmony and peace of all who are destined to live under it. Let us make our generation one of the strongest, and the brightest link, in that golden chain which is destined, I fully believe, to grapple the people of all the States to this Constitution, for ages to come. It is a great popular Constitutional Government, guarded by legislation, by law, by judicature, and defended by the whole affections of the people. No monarchical throne presses these States together; no iron chain of despotic power encircles them; they live and stand upon a Government popular in its form, representative in its character, founded upon principles of equality, and calculated, we hope, to last forever. In all its history, it has been beneficent, it has trodden down no man's liberty; it has crushed no State. Its daily respiration is liberty and patriotism; its yet youthful veins are full of enterprise, courage, and honorable love of glory and renown. It has received a vast addition of territory. Large before, the country has now, by recent events, become vastly larger. This Republic now extends, with a vast breadth, across the whole continent. The two great seas of the world wash the one and the other shore. We realize on a mighty scale, the beautiful description of the ornamental edging of the buckler of Achilles—

Now the broad shield complete the artist crowned,
With his last hand, and poured the ocean round;
In living silver seemed the waves to roll,
And beat the buckler's verge, and bound the whole.

WILLIAM H. SEWARD'S HIGHER LAW SPEECH

I AM OPPOSED TO ANY SUCH COMPROMISE, IN ANY AND ALL THE FORMS IN WHICH IT HAS BEEN PROPOSED, because, while admitting the purity and the patriotism of all from whom it is my misfortune to differ, I think all legislative compromises radically wrong and essentially vicious. They involve the surrender of the exercise of judgment and conscience on distinct and separate questions, at distinct and separate times, with the in-

Appendix, Congressional Globe, XXII, Part 1, 1st session, 31st Congress, 1849–50, from pages 262–265.

dispensable advantages it affords for ascertaining truth. They involve a relinquishment of the right to reconsider in future the decisions of the present, on questions prematurely anticipated; and they are a usurpation as to future questions of the province of future legislators.

Sir, it seems to me, as if slavery had laid its paralyzing hand upon myself, and the blood were coursing less freely than its wont through my veins, when I endeavor to suppose that such a compromise has been effected, and my utterance forever is arrested upon all the great questions, social, moral, and political, arising out of a subject so important, and as yet so incomprehensible. What am I to receive in this compromise? freedom in California. It is well; it is a noble acquisition; it is worth a sacrifice. But what am I to give as an equivalent? a recognition of a claim to perpetuate slavery in the District of Columbia; forbearance towards more stringent laws concerning the arrest of persons suspected of being slaves found in the free States; forbearance from the *proviso* of freedom in the charters of new territories. None of the plans of compromise offered, demand less than two, and most of them insist on all of these conditions. The equivalent then is, some portion of liberty—some portion of human rights in one region, for liberty in another region. But California brings gold and commerce as well as freedom. I am, then, to surrender some portion of human freedom in the District of Columbia, and in East California and New Mexico, for the mixed consideration of liberty, gold, and power on the Pacific coast.

This view of legislative compromises is not *new;* It has widely prevailed, and many of the State constitutions interdict the introduction of more than one sub-

ject into one bill submitted for legislative action.

It was of such compromises that Burke said, in one of the loftiest bursts even of his majestic parliamentary eloquence:

Far, far from the Commons of Great Britain be all manner of real vice; but ten thousand times further from them—as far as from pole to pole—be the whole tribe of spurious, affected, counterfeit and hypocritical virtues. These are the things which are ten thousand times more at war with real virtue—these are the things which are ten thousand times more at war with real duty, than any vice known by its name, and distinguished by its proper character.

Far, far from us be that false and affected candor that is eternally in treaty with crime —that half virtue, which, like the ambiguous animal that flies about in the twilight of a compromise between day and night, is, to a just man's eye, an odious and disgusting thing. There is no middle point, my Lords, in which the Commons of Great Britain can meet tyranny and oppression.

But, sir, if I could overcome my repugnance to compromises in general, I should object to this one, on the ground of the *inequality* and *incongruity* of the interests to be compromised. Why, sir, according to the views I have submitted, California ought to come in, and must come in, whether slavery stands or falls in the District of Columbia, whether slavery stands or falls in New Mexico and Eastern California, and even whether slavery stands or falls in the slave States. California ought to come in, being a free State, and under the circumstances of her conquest, her compact, her abandonment, her justifiable and necessary establishment of a constitution, and the inevitable dismemberment of the empire consequent upon her rejection. I should have voted for her admission, even if she had come as a slave State. California ought to come in, and must come in, at all events. It is, then, an independent—a paramount question. What, then, are these questions arising out of slavery, thus interposed, but collateral questions? They are unnecessary and incongruous, and therefore false issues, not introduced designedly, indeed, to defeat that great policy, yet unavoidably tending to that end.

＊　　＊　　＊

Another objection arises out of the principle on which the demand for compromise rests. That principle assumes a classification of the States as northern and southern States, as it is expressed by the honorable Senator from South Carolina, [Mr. Calhoun] but into slave States and free States, as more directly expressed by the honorable Senator from Georgia [Mr. Berrien]. The argument is, that the States are severally equal, and that these two classes were equal at the first, and that the Constitution was founded on that equilibrium—that the States being equal, and the classes of the States being equal in rights, they are to be regarded as constituting an association, in which each State, and each of these classes of States, respectively, contribute in due proportions—that the new territories are a common acquisition, and the people of these several States and classes of States, have an equal right to participate in them respectively—that the right of the people of the slave States to emigrate to the territories with their slaves, as property, is necessary to afford such a participation on their part, inasmuch as the people of the free States emigrate into the same territories with their property. And the argument deduces from this right the principle, that if Congress exclude slavery from any part of this new domain, it would be only just to set off a portion of the domain—some say south of 36° 30', others south of 34°—which should be regarded at least as free to slavery, and to be organized into slave States.

Argument, ingenious and subtle—declamation, earnest and bold—and persuasion gentle, and winning as the voice of the turtle-dove when it is heard in the land—all alike and altogether, have failed to convince me of the soundness of this principle of the compromise, or of any one of the propositions on which it is attempted to be established.

How is the original equality of the States proved? It rests on a syllogism of Vattel, as follows: All men are equal by the law of nature and of nations. But States are only lawful aggregations of individual men, who severally are equal; therefore States are equal in natural rights. All this is just and sound; but assuming the same premises, to wit: that all men are equal by the law of nature and of nations, the right of property in slaves falls to the ground; for one who is equal to the other, cannot be the owner or property of that other. But you answer that the Constitution recognizes property in slaves. It would be sufficient, then, to reply, that this constitutional recognition must be void, because it is repugnant to the law of nature and of nations. But I deny that the Constitution recognizes property in man. I submit, on the other hand, most respectfully, that the Constitution not merely does not affirm that principle, but, on the contrary, altogether excludes it.

The Constitution does not *expressly* affirm anything on the subject; all that it contains are two incidental allusions to slaves. These are—first, in the provision establishing a ratio of representation and taxation; and secondly, in the provision relating to fugitives from labor. In both cases the Constitution designedly mentions slaves, not as slaves, much less as chattels, but as *persons*. That this recognition of them as persons was designed, is historically known, and I think was never denied. I give only two of the manifold proofs. First, John Jay, in the Federalist, says:

Let the case of the slaves be considered, as it is in truth, a peculiar one. Let the compromising expedient of the Constitution be mutually adopted, which regards them as *inhabitants*, but as based below the equal level of free inhabitants, which regards the slave as divested of two fifths of the man.

Yes, sir, of two fifths, but of only two fifths—leaving still three fifths—leaving the slave still an *inhabitant*, a person, a living, breathing, moving, reasoning, immortal man.

The other proof is from the debates in the Convention. It is brief, and I think instructive:

August 28, 1787.—Mr. Butler and Mr. Pinckney moved to require fugitive slaves and servants to be delivered up like convicts.

Mr. Wilson. This would oblige the Executive of the State to do it at public expense.

Mr. Sherman saw no more propriety in the public seizing and surrendering a slave or a servant, than a horse.

Mr. Butler withdrew his proposition, in order that some particular provision might be made apart from this article.

August 29.—Mr. Butler moved to insert after article xv: "If any person bound to service or labor in any of the United States shall escape into another State, he or she shall not be discharged from such service or labor in consequence of any regulation subsisting in the State to which they escape, but shall be delivered up to the person justly claiming their service or labor."

After the engrossment, September 15, page 550, article iv, section 2, the 3d paragraph, the term "legally" was struck out,

and the words "under the laws thereof" inserted after the word "State," in compliance with the wishes of some who thought the term "legal" equivocal, and favoring the idea that slavery was legal in a *moral view*. —*Madison Debates*, pp. 487, 492.

I deem it established, then, that the Constitution does not recognize property in man, but leaves that question, as between the States, to the law of nature and of nations. That law, as expounded by Vattel, is founded in the reason of things. When God had created the earth, with its wonderful adaptations, He gave dominion over it to man—absolute human dominion. The title of that dominion, thus bestowed, would have been incomplete, if the Lord of all terrestrial things could himself have been the property of his fellowman.

The right to *have* a slave, implies the right in some one to *make* the slave; that right must be equal and mutual, and this would resolve society into a state of perpetual war. But if we grant the original equality of the States, and grant also the constitutional recognition of slaves as property, still the argument we are considering fails; because the States are not parties to the Constitution as States; it is the Constitution of the people of the United States.

But even if the States continue as States, they surrendered their equality as States, and submitted themselves to the sway of the numerical majority, with qualifications or checks—first, of the representation of three fifths of slaves in the ratio of representation and taxation; and secondly, of the equal representation of States in the Senate.

The proposition of an established classification of States, as *slave States* and *free States*, as insisted on by some, and into *northern* and *southern*, as maintained by others, seems to me purely imaginary, and of course the supposed equilibrium of those classes a mere conceit. This must be so, because, when the Constitution was adopted, twelve of the thirteen States were slave States, and so there was no equilibrium. And so as to the classification of States as northern States and southern States. It is the maintenance of slavery by law in a State, not parallels of latitude, that makes it a southern State; and the absence of this, that makes it a northern State. And so all the States, save one, were southern States, and there was no equilibrium. But the Constitution was made, not only for southern and northern States, but for States neither northern nor southern—the western States, their coming in being foreseen and provided for.

It needs little argument to show that the idea of a joint stock association, or a copartnership, as applicable even by its analogies to the United States, is erroneous, with all the consequences fancifully deduced from it. The United States are a political state, or organized society, whose end is government, for the security, welfare, and happiness, of all who live under its protection. The theory I am combating, reduces the objects of government to the mere spoils of conquest. Contrary to a theory so debasing, the preamble of the Constitution not only asserts the sovereignty to be, not in the States, but in the people, but also promulgates the objects of the Constitution:

We, the people of the United States, in order to form a *more perfect union,* establish *justice,* insure *domestic tranquility,* provide for the *common defence,* promote the GENERAL WELFARE, and secure the *blessings of liberty,* do ordain and establish this Constitution.

Objects sublime and benevolent! They exclude the very idea of conquests, to be divided either among States, or even enjoyed by them, for the purpose of securing, not the blessings of liberty, but the evils of slavery. There is a novelty in the principles of the compromise which condemns it. Simultaneously with the establishment of the Constitution, Virginia ceded to the United States her domain, which then extended to the Mississippi, and was even claimed to extend to the Pacific ocean. Congress accepted it, and unanimously devoted the domain to freedom, in the language from which the ordinance, now so severely condemned, was borrowed. Five States have already been organized on this domain, from all of which, in pursuance of that ordinance, slavery is excluded. How did it happen that this theory of the equality of States, of the classification of States, of the equilibrium of States, of the title of the States to common enjoyment of the domain, or to an equitable and just partition between them, was never promulgated, nor even dreamed of by the slave States, when they unanimously consented to that ordinance?

There is another aspect of the principle of compromise, which deserves consideration. It assumes that slavery, if not the only institution in a slave State, is at least a ruling institution, and that this characteristic is recognized by the Constitution. But *slavery* is only *one* of many institutions there—freedom is equally an institution there. Slavery is only a temporary, accidental, partial, and incongruous one; freedom, on the contrary, is a perpetual, organic, universal one, in harmony with the Constitution of the United States. The slaveholder himself stands under the protection of the latter, in common with all the free citizens of the State; but it is, moreover, an indispensable institution. You may separate slavery from South Carolina, and the

State will still remain; but if you subvert freedom there, the State will cease to exist. But the principle of this compromise gives complete ascendancy in the slave State, and in the Constitution of the United States, to the subordinate, accidental, and incongruous institution over its paramount antagonist. To reduce this claim for slavery to an absurdity, it is only necessary to add, that there are only two States in which slaves are a majority, and not one in which the slaveholders are not a very disproportionate minority.

But there is yet another aspect in which this principle must be examined. It regards the domain only as a possession, to be enjoyed, either in common or by partition, by the citizens of the old States. It is true, indeed, that the national domain is ours; it is true, it was acquired by the valor and with the wealth of the whole nation; but we hold, nevertheless, no arbitrary power over it. We hold no arbitrary authority over anything, whether acquired lawfully, or seized by usurpation. The Constitution regulates our stewardship; the Constitution devotes the domain to union, to justice, to defence, to welfare, and to liberty.

But there is a higher law than the Constitution, which regulates our authority over the domain, and devotes it to the same noble purposes. The territory is a part—no inconsiderable part—of the common heritage of mankind, bestowed upon them by the Creator of the universe. We are his stewards, and must so discharge our trust as to secure, in the highest attainable degree, their happiness. How momentous that trust is, we may learn from the instructions of the founder of modern philosophy.

No man (says Bacon) can by care-taking, as the Scripture saith, add a cubit to his stature in this little model of a man's body; but, in the great frame of kingdoms and commonwealths, it is in the power of princes or estates to add amplitude and greatness to their kingdom; for by introducing such ordinances, constitutions, and customs as are wise, they may sow greatness to their posterity and successors. But these things are commonly not observed, but left to take their chance.

This is a State, and we are deliberating for it, just as our fathers deliberated in establishing the institutions we enjoy. Whatever superiority there is in our condition and hopes, over those of any other "kingdom" or "estate," is due to the fortunate circumstance that our ancestors did not leave things to "take their chance," but that they "added amplitude and greatness" to our commonwealth, "by introducing such ordinances, constitutions, and customs as were wise." We, in our turn, have succeeded to the same responsibilities; and we cannot approach the duty before us, wisely or justly, except we raise ourselves to the great consideration of how we can most certainly "sow greatness to our posterity and successors."

And now the simple, bold, and even awful question which presents itself to us, is this: Shall we, who are founding institutions, social and political, for countless millions—shall we, who know by experience the wise and the just, and are free to choose them, and to reject the erroneous and unjust—shall we establish human bondage, or permit it, by our sufferance, to be established? Sir, our forefathers would not have hesitated an hour. They found slavery existing here, and they left it only because they could not remove it. There is not only no free State which would now establish it, but there is no slave State, which, if it had had the free alternative, as we now have, would have founded slavery. Indeed, our revolutionary predecessors had precisely the same question before them in establishing an organic law, under which the States of Ohio, Michigan, Illinois, Wisconsin, and Iowa have since come into the Union; and they solemnly repudiated and excluded slavery from those States forever. I confess that the most alarming evidence of our degeneracy, which has yet been given, is found in the fact that we even debate such a question.

Sir, there is no Christian nation, thus free to choose as we are, which would establish slavery. I speak on due consideration, because Britain, France, and Mexico have abolished slavery, and all other European States are preparing to abolish it as speedily as they can. We cannot establish slavery, because there are certain elements of the security, welfare, and greatness of nations, which we all admit, or ought to admit, and recognize as essential; and these are the security of natural rights, the diffusion of knowledge, and the freedom of industry. Slavery is incompatible with all of these, and just in proportion to the extent that it prevails and controls in any republican State, just to that extent it subverts the principle of democracy, and converts the State into an aristocracy or a despotism.

DIFFERING HISTORICAL INTERPRETATIONS OF THE GREAT DEBATE

James Schouler: THE ADMINISTRATION OF ZACHARY TAYLOR

THERE was just time left, before the Christmas holidays, for Congress to receive the President's message, dated twenty days earlier. It was brief, scarcely half the average length of his predecessor's prosy documents; a frank and faithful exposition of the national situation, replete with facts, but sparing in comment; modest—and, possibly, too much so—in what it recommended. What the President had to say of California and the new territories was most pertinent and of course absorbed attention. He favored most heartily the admission of California as a State at once with its anti-slavery constitution. As the people of New Mexico were taking steps likewise to frame a constitution after their own choice, he advised that we should await their action, and abstain from introducing those sectional topics which had produced such fearful apprehensions. This was the President's ground, and in a special message, a few weeks later, he stated it more explicitly. However its details might have varied or deserved variation, the cardinal idea was to keep the admission of California distinctly in the front as the present and pressing object of legislation, and remit all other issues involving angry recrimination between freedom and slavery to the background.

Taylor's plan was simple, sagacious, and eminently moderate. It was just and practical, and suited better than any other the general temper of the country. It avoided all Congressional extension, for the present, of the Wilmot Proviso—the point upon which the whole South at this time had become very sensitive. Northern men, surely, needed not to hazard the Union on a punctilio of expression when they had its substance. But for that very reason the plan was less acceptable to Southern members, many of whom, not satisfied with a literal concession of this kind, saw that its probable substitution was a Wilmot Proviso grafted into new State constitutions by the will of the settlers. Webster lanced the difficulty, though much too severely, when he likened the plan later to poor King Lear's proposal to shoe his horses with felt and steal behind his adversaries. This was no madman's freak, impossible of execution. The South had been wrought up to a frenzied pitch where the assertion by Congress of the Wilmot Proviso would have been resented like a blow in the face; but the vital principle of that Proviso was not to be abandoned, and it was practical statesmanship to adhere to that principle but avoid all needless and irritating assertion. This was the pith of the President's plan, and as a Southerner he understood the temper of his fellow-citizens. They were not reasoning; they were angry over their wounded honor. "My Southern blood and feelings are up," wrote one of them who had meant no treason, "and I

James Schouler, *History of the United States*, Vol. V (New York: Dodd, Mead and Company, 1891), from pp. 159–190.

feel as if I am prepared to fight at all hazards and to the last extremity."

* * *

It was on the 21st of January that the President's plan was fully stated in an executive message. On the 29th of the same month Clay proposed in the Senate his own comprehensive scheme of adjustment. California's admission, he contended, would disturb the equilibrium between free and slave States, and give to the North the most substantial benefits of the Mexican war. To meet this as well as other mutual grievances of the sections, these specific objects should be assented to: (1) The speedy admission of California, with her free-State constitution. (2) Territorial governments in New Mexico and Utah, without any express restriction upon slavery. (3 and 4) The establishment of a boundary line between Texas and New Mexico which should yield slightly to the demands of the former, at the same time paying her a money indemnity for the extinction of her claims to the rest. (5) No abolition of slavery in the District of Columbia without the assent of Maryland. (6) Slave-trade prohibition in that district, as a concession to Northern sentiment. (7) A more effective fugitive-slave law, in the interest of the South. (8) Denial to Congress of all power to interfere with the slave-trade as between slaveholding States. Such were the features of Clay's plan of compromise as embodied in his original resolutions. And except for its trivial exclusion of the hammer and auction-block from under the eyes of Congress, all its concessions favored the South; while the practical consequence of such a scheme was to obstruct free California's admission, as Clay confessed with candor, by loading the other territories on her back and

making her the scapegoat for national sins of which she was entirely innocent. There was, however, one feature in the scheme which, had Clay presented it by itself, might without opposing the wishes of the administration have passed on its independent merits; which was to buy out the Texan claims upon New Mexico, arrogant though they were, and avert that pretext for civil war. "Texas has no title," Clay argued, "but at least plausible pretensions."

Fervid with eloquence, as always, Clay appealed strongly for the Union; and yet, one must confess, with that slippery grasp of moral differences which was always his political infirmity. With the South, he argued, the question was one of interest, with the North one of principle; "but," he added fallaciously, "it is easier to make a concession of sentiment than of interest." Not even fellow-citizens from his own section, when he first spoke, inclined to uphold his plan of accommodation; many were positively set against it. Both Foote and Mason insinuated that he turned his back upon the wishes of his own section. Jefferson Davis went so far as to avow that there was but one compromise possible with the South, one ultimatum; and that was to extend the Missouri line to the Pacific, with a full legal recognition of slavery on every inch south of it. To this replied Clay with solemn emphasis: "No earthly power could induce me to vote for a specific measure introducing slavery where it has not before existed, either south or north of the Missouri line." But from that noble postulate, as we shall see, he was soon drawn, being anxious above all things to conciliate the violent and carry his point.

Clay's second speech on his resolutions showed him to best advantage. Such was the sensation he created that thousands came from Baltimore and more distant cities to hear him. Women, richly dressed, waved their fans, and smiled from the semicircle which surrounded the grave deliberators. Calhoun's chair was vacant by reason of his sickness; Webster too was absent, arguing before the Supreme Court; but most other Senators were in their places, and Buchanan, the late Secretary of State, occupied a chair next to Benton. The orator, who was still unbent with years, rose gracefully and majestically, the tallest man physically among his compeers, and renewing, as it seemed, his prime from the elixir of the occasion. Applause broke out as he stood there, which spread its magnetism to the dense crowd outside the chambers to whom he was invisible, until they lifted up such a shout that the officers of the Senate had to go out to clear the entrance. Then Clay began: his voice and enunciation clear, as of old, his action firm, and his strength for the time so great that he seemed to fling away age and all ailments by the force of his indomitable will. He enchained the attention of his hearers hour after hour as he spun the golden thread of impassioned argument. Southern opponents did not this time interrupt him. And when he had concluded, throngs of both sexes gathered round him to congratulate, and women kissed his face, unabashed by the throng of distinguished men who stood by. Surely for sympathetic eloquence and all those fascinating powers which win personal devotion, there was no civilian like Henry Clay so long as he lived. And wavering men of his section, who for weeks had hovered about the brink of disunion, felt a strong grasp which pulled them back.

The spectacle of famous oratory for this last of dramatic sessions was not ended. Other master spirits were next to appear with potent spells to save or dis-

unite the country. A few days after Clay's second speech arrived members elect to the House from California; and the news, moreover, that a State governor had been inaugurated, and Gwin and Fremont chosen by the legislature of that State to the Senate. On the 13th of the same month the President submitted to Congress an official copy of California's constitution. A cursory debate was now opened, and Senators one after another stood up to announce what each would or would not give up for the common harmony. Jefferson Davis, who had just been re-elected for a new term, made a speech against the compromise resolutions, in which he contended, as Calhoun had done, that slavery was not local, but an institution of the United States, which penetrated by its own force wherever our flag was carried. Benton confuted this theory; after showing with much learning—for he was a good Spanish scholar—that slavery had been abolished through every square acre of our Mexican conquest. Bell, of Tennessee, submitted a compromise scheme of his own.

March saw the climax of the discussion which Clay had started. Three historical speeches, all different in cast and expression, offered rallying-points for public opinion in different quarters of the Union. Calhoun, Webster, and Seward, in succession, were the speakers. Calhoun's speech, long promised and carefully written out, was the last great effort of his life. The gloom of the sick chamber in which he prepared it deepened its raven gloss; its dismal croak was of disunion. Another crowded auditory listened to that speech, on the 4th of March, which Mason, a fellow-Senator, read from the revised proof; but Calhoun was present and listened to the delivery, like some disembodied spirit reviewing the deeds of the flesh. It was a strangely haunting spectacle. The author turned half round, and listened as though all were new to him, moving not a muscle of his face, but keeping his immovable posture—pale, skinny, and emaciated though he was—with eyes partially closed, until the last words were uttered and the spell was broken. This speech made a striking and ingenious plea for the South and slave institutions; its mystic forebodings were of secession unless the South could gain something. It favored neither Clay's plan nor the President's, nor any other practicable one, as likely to save the Union. As for California, with her "impertinence" in anticipating what Congress might legislate, it wished her severed and put back into the territorial leading-strings where she belonged. It assumed that the North, where abolitionists had been so often mobbed and denounced, was hostile to the South, and with a numerical preponderance would soon crush the institution which his section felt bound to sustain. The only antidote for disunion Calhoun could propose was for the North to give the South an equal right in the newly acquired territory, cause the stipulations concerning fugitive slaves to be faithfully fulfilled, cease agitating the slavery question, and allow the Constitution to be so amended as to restore to the South substantially the power of self-protection it possessed before the equilibrium was destroyed. "If you of the North will not do this," the speech concluded, "then let our Southern States separate and depart in peace."

The next great speech was by Webster, pronounced on the 7th of March, after a silence and deliberation on the subject so profound and continuous as to give rise to the most contradictory conjectures among those who knew him best. The legislature of his State had been disposed to brace him by good Whig resolutions, such as he had favored already; but those who were deepest in Webster's confidence restrained all such expressions. Webster's mood was sullen and haughty all the winter; repelling advice, though feeling the pulse of opinion for himself. That "seventh of March speech"—an ominous style, like those ides in the Roman calendar when the stars changed their courses and great Julius fell—made an epoch in Webster's life, and in its full consequences split irreparably the Whigs of the free States. It caused the scales to fall from the eyes of many who had hitherto idolized Webster, and proved the statesman fallible. Webster was well aware, when he delivered it, that it was the most momentous effort of his life. He stood before his own crowded auditory to deliver it, arrayed carefully in his customary suit for great occasions of oratory—blue dress coat with brass buttons and buff vest. He spoke, except for the two crowning passages, which had the old majestic warmth, with more than his usual calmness and self-command; and friends and foes were agreed that while, in some respects, his opinions may have been held in suspense to the last moment, every sentence of his speech was measured, and every word premeditated.

What, then, was the tenor of that speech? "For the Union and Constitution" was Webster's own christening of it; and he consoled himself for the offence it would give to the conscience sentiment at home upon the slavery question by averring himself, now and henceforth, as "an American," "having no locality but America." Its scope was essentially to approve Clay's resolutions and compromise, though Clay's name was not once mentioned in an oration which was full of caressing compliment to

Southern men, Calhoun among the rest. Unlike Clay, it was for Webster to announce what Whigs Northern born, and with strong anti-slavery convictions like his own, would yield for national harmony; and really it did seem as if Webster yielded everything. Could anything sound nobler than those two great passages, struck from that profounder conception which makes Webster's inspiration lasting? "Peaceable secession," which foretold so clearly that Calhoun's theory was impossible, that there could be no "parting in peace" by discontented States. And that no less splendid peroration, worthy of Webster's best efforts, which adjured his hearers to "come out into the light of day and enjoy the fresh air of liberty and union." How broad, how generous, how simply strong the imagery. And yet that adjuration to "liberty and union" had not the courageous ring of that splendid reply to Hayne in other years; for the orator emerged rather from the shambles, from some cave, reeking with the blood of human sacrifice, and (to use his own words) "full of all that is horrid and horrible." Nor were the fallacious views of slavery here expressed like those which Webster had spoken out in younger years on Plymouth Rock. The speech apologized for the institution, put arguments into the mouths of slaveholders, reproached the North with unfaithfulness to constitutional vows, puffed the Wilmot Proviso aside as a useless shibboleth, and gave up the whole cause for Free Soil, as preached in 1848, no less than the violent abolitionists.

It was the tone, the bias, the coloring of this speech, above all, which made it not only wounding, but deeply exasperating, to Webster's State and section. New England was smitten in the face where she had hoped for a defence. For the great slavery problem in this country, which engaged the earnest thoughts of thousands who were honorable citizens, this speech offered no solution; for all thought upon such a subject it compressed the philosophy of a sneer. In short, the whole tenor and tone of this production were a surprise to Webster's constituents; it fell far short of the occasion; and good Whigs said, and not without good reason, that he who hitherto had led freedom's hosts fled on the day of battle.

So intent had been the orator to espouse the grievances of the South that he quite forgot some of the Northern wrongs to counterbalance, and inserted a new paragraph, on the advice of friends, when his speech was reprinted at home. And there is good reason to think that Webster wavered to the last moment in his dilemma whether to support Clay or the President. The burning words of his utterances in 1848 he could not have forgotten. Taylor stood upon the ground Webster had challenged him to occupy with him, when he last spoke upon this subject. Indeed, there is some curious testimony on this point, covering the winter of the great statesman's silence. He consulted Free Soilers like Giddings. He congratulated Winthrop of the House upon a speech the latter made in February, which pledged support to the President's policy; and that fellow-citizen, to whom he certainly owed his confidence, was dismayed at the ground his great chieftain took afterwards. Winthrop, like many others, believed the March speech, in its momentous purpose, to have been settled but shortly before it was spoken; and in the Seward family the story is handed down that Taylor's administration had verbal assurance from Webster's own lips that he would speak to support it. Be this as it may, Webster's only son received an office about the first of March—that son concerning whose disappointment the year before, Webster had opened his pent-up wrath in private so strongly to a friend. Webster, no doubt, was conservative by training and instinct, incapable of aggressive assault upon the States where slavery was already entrenched behind the Constitution. His mental struggle must have been over freedom's ordinance in the territories, and resistance to new encroachments. All that Webster has revealed of such a mental struggle is very little; but we know that he fought off all local expression from the Massachusetts Whigs, whose conscience was never stronger, and shrank from being accosted as the standard-bearer against what his mind admitted was a great national evil. Yet all this while slaveholding Whigs had reason to think that the Massachusetts lion was already in their toils. And Webster, after he had spoken, hastened to mail a copy of his speech to Ex-President Tyler, with expressions of his "cordial friendship." Friendship, one would think, was an unhappy relation to cherish towards the renegade chieftain who had elbowed Webster from his cabinet when he could not make a tool of him for annexing slave territory.

The third great speech of March was by Seward. It upheld the President's course, and pleaded for the admission of California under her free State constitution, without extraneous conditions. The young Senator from New York was already looked upon as the Mordecai in the king's gate; and Southern men blamed the President, one of themselves, for being under such influence. To this new champion of the forum listened all of the triumvirate, gazing silently while he spoke of things strange

to them. He seemed really younger than he was; a man slightly built and agile, clad in plain black; his reddish hair turning brown, but not yet mingled with gray; his compact head and curving features marked strongest in the profile. Trying, indeed, must it have been for Seward, on his first national occasion, to face potentates so famous, and yet so distrustful of him. When he first arose he spoke with hesitation, as though his heart failed him, and he seemed commonplace by comparison; but the substance of his speech was striking, and his plain features soon lighted up, until the warmth of his eloquence stirred the whole chamber. He urged broad moral principle, as one who thought the old equilibrium of the sections should never be restored. He condemned all political compromises which involved matters of the conscience; and confidently presaged the power of the American people to maintain their national integrity under whatever menace of danger. This was the speech, long commented upon, which announced the "higher law" doctrine— that higher law to which all human legislation shall conform.

Of all these famous Senatorial speeches, Seward's was by far the most profound, and worthiest of being read in a calmer age. It was full of thought and humanity, and lighted up with prophetic insight. But Calhoun, most of the Olympian trio, was galled by it. The dying statesman had glided in like a spectre on the day that Webster spoke, and taken part in a brief colloquy at the close of its magnificent peroration. More than once did he return, and when Seward spoke he sat riveted, with glassy eyeballs fixed intently upon him. And muttering what sounded like a malediction, he said to friends about him that one with such ideas of "higher law" was not the kind of man to associate with; and in that repelling mood, so fame reports, he left the accustomed chamber never to return. Calhoun died on the last day of March, an unrepentant rebel. And on his dying bed he told Toombs that he must leave to younger men the task of carrying out his plans.

Benton favored the President's plan, and alone among the Southern Senators sustained it heartily. Experience in the Jackson times had given him confidence that an unflinching Executive could override a disputatious Senate. Various causes were turning this border statesman to an independent course in politics, whose end was orphanage. The question, after all, concerned Whig policy. It was a perilous crisis.

Had Clay and Webster—or had either of them—stood by their President, history might have vindicated a policy against which rebellion had no just cause for appeal. Sooner or later California's admission as a free State must have been granted if she was to remain a national prize at all, and in all other respects— except the boundary issue with Texas— the territorial question might have been adjourned for twenty years. . . .

*　　*　　*

President Taylor seemed likely to command the field. The loyal people preferred his plan, and the most influential Whig presses sustained it. An event happened in June which disheartened the disunionists. A convention of delegates from the slaveholding States met in Nashville on the 3rd of that month pursuant to a call, Judge Sharkey of Mississippi presiding. Ultra slaveholders had hoped that this body would present to the country the solemn alternative of secession or compliance with their extreme demands. But the bones of Jackson and Calhoun mouldered in graves hundreds of miles apart; no new leader of the disunion party had yet arisen; the attendance was unexpectedly thin, and instead of fierce thunderbolts were subdued mutterings. A political movement much dreaded while Calhoun was alive collapsed in ridicule. Southern tyros in treason sought refuge in Clay's "rickety ark" of compromise; but the more that tendency was perceptible on one side, the more closely, on the other, did loyalty lean to the side of the President. The House struggled through obstruction to pass a bill for the simple admission of California as a free State, and it took the best brains of slaveholding tacticians to stave off a vote so that the Senate might have precedence.

The real seat of danger was New Mexico, where the people were already in motion to form a free-State constitution and apply for admission as California had done. Southern ultras as a last resort urged Texas to take the bold leap and secure her prey, pledging themselves to sustain her pretensions at all hazards. They hoped thus to wrest New Mexico from freedom's arms, or, if opposed, plunge the Union in civil war. That movement was rash and premature, and the President met it without flinching. He had no thought of settling the boundary question arbitrarily; at the same time he considered it a question not between Texas and New Mexico, while the latter remained a territory, but between Texas and the United States, the guardian and owner of that territory. In that sense he meant to protect the boundary line which Mexico had defined by the treaty of Guadalupe-Hidalgo until by the intervention of Congress or a suit in the federal courts the dispute was definitely settled. The war which brought us New Mexico cost the Union millions upon millions of dollars and many thousand lives; it cost Texas, as such, nothing; and the cession from the parent republic by dint of conquest made no mention whatever of Texas as an interested claimant. New Mexico, indeed, was an ancient province of the Spanish dominion, having its own homogeneous population, though a small one; nor had Texas ever invaded that Sante Fé region without being repulsed.

In November, 1849, Taylor, through his Secretary of War, instructed Colonel Monroe, our military commandant there, to aid the inhabitants of New Mexico to form a State government. As to the disputed boundary, he superseded his predecessor's orders, so far as to direct the existing status to be maintained until Congress could dispose of the subject. Texas played a bold hand, as the only one that could win the stakes. A Texan militia force penetrated New Mexico by the El Paso route and summoned Colonel Monroe to aid in establishing Texan jurisdiction over the region. Monroe declined, but proclaimed neutrality upon the boundary dispute. The inhabitants next bestirred themselves after the example of the Californians, though on a much smaller scale. Monroe, as military governor, acted as General Riley had done, and in April called a convention of delegates to form a State constitution.

By peaceful process a suit in our Supreme Court might have settled the Texan claim of boundaries. Recourse to compact, on the other hand, was a feature of Clay's scheme for log-rolling the moralities; nor was that, perhaps, an unfair solution of the Texan difficulty, had Clay but placed it apart upon its separate pedestal of merit. For all that Texas blustered so, she feared the President, and her disloyal contumacy could be bought off. It was the license Congress

had given Texas in 1845 to form new slave States from her jurisdiction, which led rebellious slaveholders to plunge that jurisdiction into new directions. The threats grew louder and more insolent when New Mexico was seen organizing her own people on freedom's side and sinking the old federal equilibrium to a deeper perdition. Taylor maintained official reserve, but he welcomed none the less those popular omens. The same menaces which drove our chief civilians to truckling stirred him to put rebellion down. He disliked the whole compromise of iniquities, wished California's admission granted upon its own merits, and the integrity of the Union maintained at every hazard. "I would rather," he said impetuously to Webster, "have California wait, than bring in all the territories on her back."

Fellow-slaveholders from the Gulf States, men who thought it sacred honor to band their interests together, tried to drive the President from this attitude. At a secret meeting held by the Southern Whigs of Congress, a committee was appointed to remonstrate with him, threatening, if need be, their opposition. This was about the last of June. The delegates found him stubborn, and their interview at the White House was a stormy one. Would he pledge himself to sign no bill with the Wilmot Proviso in it? The old warrior replied that he would sign any constitutional bill that Congress presented him. Next they threatened to break up the Union. "Southern officers," added one of them "will refuse to obey your orders if you send troops to coerce Texas." "Then," responded Taylor, in high excitement, "I will command the army in person; and any man who is taken in treason against the Union I will hang as I did the deserters and spies at Monterrey." The commitee withdrew crestfallen; for they knew the general was inflexible to obstinacy where, as in the present case, he believed himself right. "What are you doing with that 'Omnibus Bill'?" asked the President of Hannibal Hamlin, a Democratic senator from Maine, who entered the room as they passed out. "I believe the bill wrong in principle, Mr. President," was Hamlin's reply, "and I am trying to do what I can to defeat it." "Stand firm," said the President; "don't yield; it means disunion, and I am pained to learn that we have disunion men to deal with; disunion is treason." And with a blunt expletive which gave emphasis to his feelings, he added that he would treat traitors as they deserved.

A military force had actually organized in Texas to invade New Mexico and annex that territory by violence. To counteract the design, Taylor ordered Colonel Monroe to be reinforced, and directed that any attempt from Texas to exercise armed jurisdiction should be repelled. Crawford, the Secretary of War, whose leaning favored Stephens and Toombs, his personal friends, was appalled when directed to issue such an order and said he could not sign it. "Then," said Taylor, firmly, "I will sign the order myself."

The worst of civil collision and bloodshed is that the spirit of accommodation may be put to flight. And yet the danger at Santa Fé, the loss which the Union might apprehend in ultimate results, was most likely exaggerated by the great Senators who so loftily measured their intellects against Taylor's downright common sense. Indeed, when we consider the terrible conflict which it cost, years later, to vindicate against these imperious slaveholders the supremacy of the Union, the historian cannot but confess a tingling wish that, on any further provo-

cation from Texas, our conqueror of Buena Vista had taken the field and thrashed her and her traitorous allies as they deserved. But while discipline would have been salutary, such extremities were not likely to have resulted from an attitude of national self-respect in this frontier dispute. The aggressors would have had the greater share of the difficulty; Texas would have failed against Santa Fé as she had failed before. All that our regulars had to do was to stand on the defensive and uphold New Mexico in her autonomy and the will of her inhabitants, until Congress acted.

Here of a sudden the dark curtain drops as the situation nears a climax. The hot July sun saw Congress still in angry vaporing over the new legacy of territories, and the public business was retarded. In the Senate the sweating task was the Omnibus bill; in the House the untrammelled admission of California. A peremptory letter reached the President from the governor of Texas asking to be informed whether the resistant attitude of New Mexico had his sanction. Almost simultaneously came tidings unofficial of Monroe's proclamation and the convention which was about to form a State. Cass, in the Senate, always ready to turn a popular penny with the South, ranted about military usurpation and proposed to cut the New Mexican policy short. In the House the President's enemies brought up the Galphin claim. Each subject was used to weaken the President in his course by imputing personal dishonor. Both Houses adjourned over the 4th, on which day the President and his suite attended a patriotic celebration on the ground where the national monument was begun. Taylor never again appeared in public. Imprudent exposure to the hot sun, followed by imprudent diet, brought on toward night an attack of cholera morbus. Medical aid was not summoned as promptly as it should have been, and a life most needful to the people hung the next day by a thread.

A messenger now arrived at the White House with the constitution which New Mexico had adopted in convention on the 25th of May, setting the boundaries of that territory as a new State and of course excluding slavery. Taylor was ill in bed; but a special cabinet meeting was held by night at Clayton's house, in which the majority agreed to stand by the new State and the wishes of its inhabitants at all hazards. That was the President's own desire, and a stirring message to Congress would have followed. A reconstruction of the cabinet was now quite necessary, for Crawford's dissent was plainly manifested. The Galphin claim, moreover, supplied its special reasons. Worry and new responsibilities aggravated the President's symptoms which turned soon into a fever. Even in his sick chamber the old warrior had been warned by Southern extremists that unless he took sides with slave interests they would vote to censure him. They could not carry their point. On the 8th the House, adopting the resolution of an investigating committee on the Galphin claim, censured the Secretary of the Treasury, and reflected severely upon Crawford; a proposal to censure the President failed. It was known the next afternoon that the President was dangerously ill, and both Houses adjourned in consequence. Taylor died that same evening. His last words murmured a defence of motives which had been outraged while he lay struggling for life; "I have endeavored," he said, "to do my duty."

Even those who had lent a hand in the torture felt sympathy and respect for the brave old man who had died on the rack of official responsibility. No one could now deny the purity of his intentions. A second Whig funeral went sadly forth from the White House. Clay, Cass, Webster and Benton were together among the pall bearers. The slow and solemn procession down Pennsylvania Avenue revived the associations of Taylor's military fame. Plumes of various colors waved; white, red, blue, and green marked the alternating costumes of military companies which filed with reversed arms to the brass music of the dirge. Chief among the mounted army officers towered the superb figure of General Scott, who lent his reconciling presence to these last obsequies. Duncan's light artillery was in line, which, as tradition claimed, fired the first cannon and the last in the battles of the Mexican War. And behind the sumptuous funeral car was led "old Whitey," the war horse of the dead President, richly caparisoned, but with saddle empty and never to be filled again. Other pageants, which imitated this real one, expressed the people's grief in all the chief cities of the Union.

Zachary Taylor was the first of American Presidents whose choice rested solely upon a military reputation disconnected altogether from civil pursuits. And the only errors of his administration —which, after all, were unimportant— should be ascribed to his inexperience in public affairs and his unacquaintance with public men; time would have corrected them had he lived to round out his term. His cabinet was not all it should have been, and while he was on the point of changing it death intervened, and the regret remains that he had not changed it before. In the higher aims of domestic, as well as foreign policy, he showed the best qualities of an administrator; being wise, temperate, sincere, honest as the day, more than loyal to the Union, because he loved it and would have laid down his life in its defence. He was simple in habits, frank in manners, with a genuineness which impressed all who came in contact with him, and a firmness that shunned no danger. Though not by genius or habit a statesman, he saw more clearly the bold headlands of national policy through the mists that were gathering, than the wisest and most world-renowned of our statesmen who scarcely condescended to him and thought their vision better. Nor did it take him many months to discern that what the country wished and needed was not pacification nor the plausible bargain of principles, but loyal acquiescence in nature and the right. A slaveholder himself, he yet felt that slavery ought not to extend farther. A soldier of the Union, he stood ready to lead the Union forces in his own person if his own section rebelled, and to pour out his blood in defence of the flag.

Personal example is, after all, the greatest force which can elevate or degrade a government; and the best of personal examples is that of honest patriotism striving to be right. Taylor, while he lived, inspired firmness for freedom's cause, and he was the one man before whom the false idealists of a slave confederacy quailed with fear. Naturally, then, he endeared himself to the common people, and had he lived there is little doubt that he would have carried the policy he had at heart. It was the most practical; it depended the least upon assertion by Congress. But the key of the territorial situation was lost with the warrior who grasped it. The saying had long been current, "General Taylor never surrenders"; and his first surrender was to death. His last appearance in life was fitly on the anniversary of his country's independence. His last official act was to proclaim the new compact with Great Britain. That grim conqueror, who had never checked his military renown, forbade him the proof of statesmanship, and his monument must remain an unfinished shaft.

Richard N. Current: DANIEL WEBSTER AND THE UNION

IN the winter of 1849–1850 the crisis came which Daniel Webster had prophesied would come if the United States should take any territory from Mexico. The new President, Zachary Taylor, for all the slaves he owned on his Louisiana plantation, demanded that Congress let California join the Union as a free state, and Southern hotheads swore that their own states would go out if California thus came in. Meanwhile, to expand the area of slavery, they backed the Texan imperialists who claimed much of New Mexico as a part of Texas. Over this boundary question a civil war seemed likely to break out, with Northerners rallying to the support of New Mexico and free soil.

To save the Union, the aging compromiser Henry Clay offered his last great compromise. Admit California with an antislavery constitution, he recommend-

Richard N. Current, *Daniel Webster and the Rise of National Conservatism* (Boston: Little, Brown and Company, 1955), pp. 158–171. Reprinted by permission of Little, Brown and Co. Copyright, 1955, by Richard N. Current.

ed, and settle the boundary dispute in favor of New Mexico. Do even more for the North: abolish the slave trade (though not slavery itself) in the District of Columbia. But compensate Texas by assuming her public debt, and reassure the South by passing a law more effective than the existing one for the capture and return of escaping slaves. Forget the Wilmot Proviso: say nothing about slavery in organizing the territories of New Mexico and Utah.

As between the plan of Taylor, who refused to consider tying California with the other issues, and the proposals of Clay for a general settlement, where would Webster stand?

Many antislavery people in the North hoped that he would stand with the cause of liberty. One of these people, a Unitarian preacher in Philadelphia, reminded him "how Slavery has *interfered* and is *interfering*, not with property, but with the rights, with the inmost hearts of freemen, making them its tools and supporters," and begged him to make "in that grand and simple way" of his a speech "*stating the great case.*"

His friends the New York merchants also opposed concessions to the South, at first, but early in 1850 they changed their attitude. They feared the loss of their profitable Southern trade when Southerners began to talk of seceding or, even without secession, boycotting Northern goods. In February the merchants called a mass meeting of New Yorkers "irrespective of party" to demonstrate in favor of "sustaining Mr. Clay's compromise" as the best way of achieving "the permanent settlement of the great questions now agitating the nation."

The businessmen of Boston did not agree so well among themselves or act so decisively. "They would favor any man

and any speech which would settle the slavery question and leave commerce unthreatened and unimpaired," one newspaper said, as trading remained slow on the local securities and cotton markets. Millowners, waiting impatiently for a tariff increase, now that the Whigs were in power, could expect none until Congress somehow had disposed of the vexing territorial issues.

"What say our friends in Boston?" Webster asked his scholarly and aristocratic Massachusetts colleague, Representative Robert C. Winthrop, on the latter's return to Washington after a visit home. "I thought them satisfied with the President's policy," Winthrop replied, "and not disposed to press matters to a dangerous pass upon the Wilmot Proviso." This was not very helpful advice, for (to judge from what Southerners were saying) the President's policy itself, if upheld by Congress, would press matters to a dangerous pass.

One group of moneyed men, the holders of debt certificates issued by the former Republic of Texas, felt a special interest in the passage of at least part of the Clay compromise. If the Federal government should take over the Texan debt, their speculation would turn out well. Many of the speculators were, in the words of the banker Jay Cooke, "influential northern men."

Northern property owners as a whole had a tremendous stake in the preservation of peace and union, if some of the Southerners were to be believed. Against the "centrifugal tendencies of locofocoism," of radical Democracy, Northern conservatives must ally themselves with the planters of the South, or so a Florida congressman declared (March 5, 1850). The Union, he told his fellow Whigs from the North, was indispensable to them. "To you it may be necessary to save you from the effects of Socialism, Agrarianism, Fanny Wrightism, Radicalism, Dorrism, and Abolitionism. The *conservatism of slavery* may be necessary to save you from the thousand destructive *isms* infecting the social organization of your section." A dozen years earlier John C. Calhoun had said essentially the same thing.

The Whig party, the party of big businessmen and big slaveholders, long had been the vehicle of conservatism. But the national conservatism of Webster and the North had never harmonized completely with the local conservatism of most of the planters in the South. The growth of antislavery feeling among Northern Whigs made the existing political alliance less and less attractive to Southern party members. Now, with Taylor pointing one way and Clay another, the Whig party seemed near the point of dissolution, and with the loss of this planter-capitalist axis would go a mainstay of the conservative cause, to say nothing of Webster's presidential hopes.

There was no "serious danger," Webster kept telling himself and others as the winter weeks went by. "If, on our side, we keep cool, things will come to no dangerous pass," he said as late as February 16.

Before long he changed his mind, and for good reasons. One by one the Southern states appointed delegates to an all-Southern convention to meet at Nashville in the summer and presumably make plans for a concerted secession movement. The Mississippi legislature, when naming its delegate (March 6), also appropriated two hundred thousand dollars to be used, "in the event of the passage of the Wilmot Proviso," for "necessary measures for protecting the state," that is, for war.

Meanwhile the Southerners in Congress, Whigs and Democrats combining in a sectional bloc, filibustered against the admission of California and demonstrated their power to obstruct not only the President's plan but all legislation of whatever kind. Webster knew most of the Southern senators well, and they showed him the letters they were receiving from their constituents, letters which supported the "most ultra" opinions of the politicians. He came to believe that secession and civil war were real and imminent possibilities.

"I am nearly broken down with labor and anxiety," he confessed to his son (February 24). "I know not how to meet the present emergency, or with what weapons to beat down the Northern and Southern follies, now raging in equal extremes."

One thing Webster could do was to make a speech, and he determined to do so, "to make an honest truth-telling speech and a Union speech." While preparing it he conferred privately with various Southern senators, including Calhoun, but no one knew precisely what he was going to say. His Massachusetts colleague Winthrop assumed that he would agree essentially with the administration, and the Washington correspondent of the Boston *Advertiser* predicted (March 4) that he would "take a large view of the state of things" and endorse the principle of the Taylor plan. Like many other Whigs, Webster was trying in fact to ignore the differences between Taylor and Clay, no doubt intending thereby to obscure the party rift.

On March 4 Calhoun, dying of tuberculosis, started to read a speech, then had to sit while it was read for him. He indicated that the Clay compromise was insufficient to secure the interests of the South. The North, he charged, had out-stripped the South in population and power because of unfair actions of the Federal government, because of tariffs, land laws, and expenditures on internal improvements. Political parties in the North, catering to the fanaticism of abo-litionists, were fast becoming abolition-ized, and the Northern people were be-ing convinced that slavery was a sin. In these circumstances disunionism could not be overcome by cries of "the Union, the glorious Union" (Webster's stock in trade) any more than illness could be cured by cries of "health, glorious health." The South must have constitu-tional guarantees. In a work to be pub-lished posthumously, Calhoun was pro-posing a constitutional amendment giv-ing the United States a dual presidency, one president to be elected by the North and another by the South, each with an independent veto. So far as he was con-cerned, the alternative for the South was secession, to him a perfectly constitu-tional and peaceable remedy.

On March 7 Webster rose on the Sen-ate floor, his face unusually stern as he stood for a moment and passed a hand across his forehead. "I wish to speak to-day, not as a Massachusetts man, nor as a Northern man, but as an American," he said in a conversational tone, low but clear. "I speak today for the preserva-tion of the Union." Then he launched up-on his last great performance on the senatorial stage, his gestures becoming increasingly vigorous, his voice swelling till at times the chandeliers seemed to vibrate with his words.

He pled for tolerance. As between the two sections, slavery indeed had become an ethical and even a religious issue, he said. He, for one, believed that slavery was an evil, and Southerners themselves had thought so once. Their opinions had been influenced by their interests: "it was the COTTON interest that gave a new desire to promote slavery." Any-how, the problem of ethics was too com-plex to be solved by those who "deal with morals as with mathematics" and "think that what is right may be distin-guished from what is wrong with the precision of an algebraic equation." Man's moral duties were numerous and conflicting; "too eager a pursuit" of one of them might lead to violation of others, to disregard of St. Paul's admonition not to "do evil that good may come." There were many evils in the world besides slavery, and one of the worst of them was war.

Having thus dismissed ethical abso-lutism, Webster proceeded to review and to appraise the specific grievances of both the South and the North.

Southerners like Calhoun charged that "certain operations of the government" had accounted for "the more rapid growth of the North than the South." There was perhaps some truth in this, Webster conceded, but he said it was even more certain that the government had "promoted the increase of the slave interest and the slave territory of the South," as in the acquisition of Florida, Louisiana, and especially Texas.

"Now, as to California and New Mex-ico," he went on, "I hold slavery to be excluded from those territories by a law even superior to that which admits and sanctions it in Texas." This was the law of nature, of physical geography, he said. Though peonage existed in the lands recently acquired from Mexico, African slavery of the kind familiar in the Southern states could never be suc-cessfully implanted there. Therefore, Webster declared, he would not vote for any prohibition (such as the Wilmot

Proviso) in a bill for organizing a New Mexican territorial government. "I would not take pains uselessly to reaffirm an ordinance of nature, nor to re-enact the will of God." To do so would only be to "wound the pride" of the Southern people.

Another complaint of the South was the agitation of antislavery societies in the North. These societies, Webster said, had done more harm than good even for the slaves themselves. In the Southern reaction against abolitionism "the bonds of the slaves were bound more firmly than before, their rivets were more strongly fastened." Another complaint was "the violence of the Northern press." Against this, however, Southerners could not look to the Federal government for a remedy. "With all its licentiousness and all its evil, the entire and absolute freedom of the press is essential to the preservation of government on the basis of a free constitution."

The South did have one "solid grievance," one with "just foundation," one "within the redress of the government." Northerners had shown "a disinclination to perform fully their constitutional duties in regard to persons bound to service who have escaped into the free states," said Webster. "In that respect the South, in my judgment, is right and the North is wrong."

But Northerners also had grounds for complaint against the South. They complained, with reason, of the fact that Southerners no longer regarded slavery as an evil but now regarded it as "an institution to be cherished, and preserved, and extended." Southerners even said that their slaves were better off than Northern workers. This was an insult to a whole people, Webster implied. "Why, who are the laboring people of the North? They are the whole North."

Turning to the question of remedies, Webster said that grievances on either side, so far as they arose from law, could be redressed and ought to be. So far as grievances depended on opinion, they could not be removed by legislation. "All that we can do is to endeavor to allay the agitation, and cultivate a better feeling and more fraternal sentiments between the South and the North."

As for secession, it was no remedy at all. "There can be no such thing as a peaceable secession," said Webster, contradicting Calhoun. "I see that it must produce war, and such a war as I will not describe, *in its twofold character*" (a hint of slave uprisings). Physically, the North and the South could not separate, least of all in the valley of the Mississippi, the home of the future strength of America.

Webster had one last remark, one afterthought, and here at the end he came to the heart of the nation's dilemma, to the question of slavery itself and "the mode of its extinguishment or melioration." He confessed he had nothing to recommend. He could only say that if any gentleman from the South should propose a scheme, "to be carried on by this government upon a large scale, for the transportation of free colored people to any colony or any place in the world," he would support it wholeheartedly no matter what the cost.

When he had finished, the crowd in the Senate chamber roared its applause, while hundreds pushed their way to his desk to shake his hand and give him their fervent thanks. But the ghostlike Calhoun, as soon as he could make himself heard, feebly expressed his vehement dissent, saying: "No, Sir, the Union *can* be broken." Webster admitted that it could be, but insisted: "That is *revolution*—that is revolution!" In a few minutes the two old antagonists, still respectful of one another, weary after a whole generation of debate, ceased their colloquy.

Though Webster in his speech had mentioned neither Taylor's nor Clay's proposals as such, it could be taken only as an endorsement of those of Clay. Not that he expected, by the sheer force of his argument, to convert Calhoun or other dissenters among his Senate colleagues. He did hope to reach the American people, to influence them, and through them the Congress, in favor of compromise.

Some of his Whig colleagues cautioned him that, if it went to the country just as he had delivered it, the speech would react against the party in every state above the Potomac. So, before publication, he revised it so as to make his lists of Southern and Northern grievances somewhat more balanced. He discreetly struck out a passage in which he had said the money collected by the abolitionists, if rightly spent, would have purchased the freedom of every slave in Maryland. To his list of Northern grievances he added an item concerning the arrest and imprisonment of free colored seamen on Yankee ships visiting Southern ports.

Once the speech was ready in pamphlet form, he franked thousands of copies from Washington while his business friends distributed tens of thousands from Boston and New York. "I do not care what a portion of the press may say," he wrote to one of his friends, "if we can only get the speech into the hands of the people."

Among the most important people of New York the speech proved to be an instant success. The price of United States bonds, which had been falling before March 7, rose sharply thereafter on the metropolitan exchange. Lewis Tappan, one of a tiny abolitionist minority among the businessmen, reported with disgust that "merchants," "brokers," "monied men," and "owners of bank, railroad, and manufacturing stocks" continually quoted excerpts from Webster's address. In individual letters and in one letter signed by several hundred they thanked him for his great effort. "Its tranquillizing effect upon public opinion has been wonderful," one writer said. As a more concrete token of their gratitude a group of businessmen presented to their favorite statesman a handsome gold watch and chain.

From New England he received other commendatory mail, along with it a public letter bearing the signatures of several hundred prominent Bostonians: merchants, scholars, professional men, ministers of the gospel. Many Yankees, however, withheld their praise. Even some of the manufacturers, such as Linus Childs, an official of the Lowell mills, were inclined at first to disapprove of Webster and of compromise. But he could use on them an argument as powerful as any in his speech itself. They desired a new tariff, and they could not get one without the votes of Southern Whigs. These Southerners demanded a price for their aid. "They will not give a single vote for the tariff until this slavery business is settled," Webster reported (May 29) to one of his Boston intimates, Peter Harvey. "A very leading individual among them told Mr. Childs yesterday that, so far as depended on him, the Lowell mills might and should stop, unless the North quit this violence of abuse—and showed a disposition to be reasonable in the present exciting questions."

The New England abolitionists, unmoved by economic considerations, kept flailing Webster on account of his speech. The editor of the *Liberator,* William Lloyd Garrison, condemned him as "the great apostate," and the "good gray poet" John Greenleaf Whittier anathematized him as a man whose soul had fled and whose honor had died on March 7, 1850. Somehow the reformers managed to see him as one who lately had been with them, then suddenly had turned renegade.

In truth, he never had espoused their views of slavery, though he always had considered it a moral and social evil, both before and after the firsthand knowledge he gained on his Southern trips in 1847 and 1849. He assumed that after a century or so not only slave labor but Negro labor would disappear from the South, which then would become "a most agreeable region." Pending that happy day he remained, like most Northern politicians of his time, a strict legalist and constitutionalist. Slavery within the Southern states was to him a fact, a disagreeable fact, which the Constitution recognized and with which the Federal government had no right to interfere.

On one point he did reverse himself in the Seventh of March address. Earlier, from the Missouri controversy on, he repeatedly had expressed his fear that slavery, if unhindered, would expand westward even to the Pacific. In 1848, when the Democratic presidential candidate, Lewis Cass, assured Northern voters that slavery could not, for geographical reasons, take root in New Mexico and California, Webster undertook to refute him. After the Seventh of March address Senator Stephen A. Douglas, himself the chief engineer of compromise in 1850, asked ironically why the Massachusetts statesman was so late in discovering the ordinance of nature which interdicted slavery in those territories.

Having belatedly discovered the natural ordinance, Webster stuck manfully to it and boldly denied the charges of inconsistency which came from abolitionists as well as Democrats like Douglas. The question of slavery in the territories, he said in the Senate, in vindication of his Seventh of March address, was "a mere abstraction." He was confident that such an abstraction would not deflect his fellow citizens from the pursuit of their real and substantial economic interests. Commerce, navigation, the fisheries, manufactures, all were suffering because of the sectional disturbance and the congressional impasse. "I cannot conceive," said Webster, "that these great interests would be readily surrendered by the businessmen of the country, the laboring community of the Northern states, to abstractions, to naked possibilities, to idle fears that evils may ensue if a particular abstract measure [the Wilmot Proviso] is not passed. Men must live; to live, they must work."

But he continued to receive denunciations from Northern reformers, who lived by works as well as by work, who pursued abstract ideals in disregard of economic interests. "When I see gentlemen from my own part of the country, no doubt from motives of the highest character and for the most conscientious purposes, not concurring in any of these great questions with myself," he confessed in the Senate, "I am aware that I am taking on myself an uncommon degree of responsibility." Yet, he said, he could not depart from his own convictions. "My object is peace. My object is reconciliation."

His object was achieved, though imperfectly and only temporarily. He did not succeed in silencing all the "agitators, North and South," or all the "local ideas, North and South," but he helped to rally a majority in both sections to a renewed sense of nationality and of the need for sectional give and take. He did much to create a public spirit in which

the Compromise of 1850 could finally be passed and the secession movement of that summer headed off.

Herbert Agar: CALHOUN AND THE MEANING OF 1850

TAYLOR had been opposed to dodging the issue presented by the Wilmot Proviso. In this he was supported by John C. Calhoun, who also did not want a compromise. Calhoun pressed for a final decision as to where the South stood. Superficially, the problem of the new territory seemed to have settled itself by 1850, for by that time New Mexico was known to be a dry land where no slaveholder could prosper, and California had declared her desire to be a free state. But Calhoun was looking to the future. He countered the Wilmot Proviso with the doctrine that Congress had no power to prohibit slavery in the territories, since slaves were common-law property. It was Congress's duty, he said, to protect the lawful property of American citizens, not to take their property away from them. If this doctrine were accepted (and in 1857 it was endorsed by the Supreme Court), the Missouri Compromise of 1820, which prohibited slavery in the territories north of 36° 30′, would become null and void.

Calhoun knew he would raise a storm in the North; but he wished to force the issue, being prepared for one of two results: secession (before the North was too strong to be resisted), or a constitutional amendment which would insure what he called "the rule of the concurrent majority." He wished to make certain that the South, which was already

heavily outnumbered, could never be subjected to the domination of a numerical majority resident elsewhere. One way to accomplish this, he believed, would be to create a dual Executive: one President elected by the North and another by the South, each with a legislative veto. If this were deemed impractical, the South would accept any constitutional change which made sectional compromise a necessity.

Such compromise, Calhoun felt, was the dominant theme in American political life, and the unique contribution of the United States to the political thought of the free world; but the South could no longer count on the political good sense of the North to insure compromise. The ravings of anti-slavery fanatics had clouded that good sense and the South must now insist on a form of protection which was written into the constitutional bond. This was her last chance. The North was far more wealthy than the South and far more populous. In a few years the railways would have built a new Northwest, tied to the Northeast by lines of commerce and by a common aversion to the "peculiar institution" of slavery. When that happened, the North would win final control of the government at Washington and would reinstate all the Hamiltonian policies, meanwhile interfering in every possible way with the slave sys-

Herbert Agar, *The Price of Union* (Boston: Houghton Mifflin Company, 1950), pp. 328–334. Reprinted by permission of Houghton Mifflin Company.

tem. To Calhoun this meant the doom of Southern agriculture and Southern life. If Southerners waited for secession until all this had happened, they would find themselves too weak, and would be constrained to remain in the Union under Northern domination. Now was the time to force a decision. If Union sentiment in the North was strong enough to secure a constitutional amendment protecting the South forever against exploitation, so much the better. That was the one compromise the South could afford to accept. The argument was logical, but fatally doctrinaire and unbending.

Unfortunately for Calhoun's plans, a very different compromise was accepted. Henry Clay, who had patched up the sectional quarrel in 1820, and again in 1833, returned to the Senate to face the new crisis and produced his last and greatest effort. In January, 1850, he brought forward compromise resolutions containing prizes and bitter pills for both sides. California was to be admitted at once as a free state, and the slave trade in the District of Columbia was to be stopped. Those were the Northern prizes. They were balanced by two other resolutions: that the rest of the land taken from Mexico was to be organized into territories with no provision as to slavery or its absence, and that a more strict fugitive-slave law was to be passed. A week later Clay defended the proposals in two of his finest speeches. He begged the North to understand the South's pride and the South's fears, and to accept the substance of the Wilmot Proviso without insisting that it be written into law. He begged the South to remember the benefits of Union, and not to forget that secession must mean war—"furious, bloody, implacable, exterminating." The millions who lived in the upper Missis-

sippi Valley, he said, would never permit the mouth of that river to be held by a foreign power. Throughout the long debate he returned to these points disarmingly and beguilingly. It was obvious why the public had loved him beyond all his contemporaries. In July he made the last great speech of his career.

Early in March Calhoun made his reply to the proposals. He was a dying man, and his cause was dying with him. He was so weak that he had to sit grimly watching while his speech was read by Senator Mason of Virginia. In the early days of the Union, he wrote, there had been an equal distribution of power between the North and the South. That equality was gone. In wealth and population the North had forged ahead, and the disparity would grow greater. The change had not come for natural reasons, but because of three pernicious policies of the federal government: first, the exclusion of slavery from most of the territories (under the Northwest Ordinance and the Missouri Compromise), with the result that the Southern economic system had been deprived of its proper chance to spread; second, the protective tariff, making artificially high prices for what the South had to buy, and subsidizing the Northern factory; third, the consolidation of power in the hands of the federal government, with the result that any regional majority which took charge at Washington would find an all-too-efficient weapon for oppression.

To these old wrongs a new grievance had been added: the anti-slavery agitation which openly sought to overturn the social system of the South. Unless scotched at once, this must grow stronger as the North grew stronger, until the South was forced to choose between abolition and secession.

And why should the South be forever on the defensive? The South was not seeking to impose adverse economic conditions on other regions; she was only seeking to keep other regions from imposing such conditions upon herself. The South was not trying to change the social system of Boston, or to improve the lot of wage-slaves in the factories of Fall River; the South was asking to be let alone.

Henry Clay's compromise met none of the Southern grievances. The North had taken the offensive, and that offensive must cease. If the South were given protection against exploitation or interference from without, the Union could endure forever, and for the good of all. If the South were denied this protection, she must secede.

Until the publication of his posthumous books, this was the last word from Calhoun. He died within the month. He is said to have died murmuring, "The South! The poor South! God knows what will become of her!" One of the South's devoted sons commented in 1939:

What has become of her? God knows! She went out to battle and she fell. She has lain in economic bondage longer than the republic had lasted when Calhoun was in his prime. She has felt the lash of the task-master, and has made bricks without straw. She has been perverse, and forward, and indomitable, foul and magnificent. She has produced Robert E. Lee and Huey Long, *Deep River* and *Tobacco Road*, John Wilkes Booth and Sergeant York, Woodrow Wilson and *The Memphis Blues*. In the matter of Negro enfranchisement she has defied the Constitution of the United States and she has flung her sons by thousands on the bayonets of its enemies. She has given us lessons in lynching and courtesy. Distracted, violent and tender, she is filled with loveliness and horror and drives her sons to revile while they adore her.

The decisive speech was made by Webster on the seventh of March. New England would never accept a new and more punitive Fugitive Slave Act unless it were backed by the whole power of Webster's prestige. And if the Fugitive Slave Act were rejected, the South would reject the rest of Clay's measures and Calhoun would have his way. Webster's first sentence showed that he favored the proposals: "I speak today for the preservation of the Union. Hear me for my cause." This speech, and the arduous subsequent debates, were to be his last great effort also. The speech was given added dignity by the knowledge that the men of letters and the younger men of politics in the North would turn on Webster and call him traitor for recommending the Compromise. Once again the Senate was under the spell of that conquering presence. Old age had destroyed none of Webster's impressiveness; and when, with a weakened voice but undiminished oratory, he pleaded for conciliation in the name of patriotism, it must have been hard even for a Southerner to remember the reasoning of Calhoun. "No speech more patriotic or evincing a higher degree of moral courage had ever been made in Congress," writes Professor Nevins. "For once Webster rose to the highest level of statesmanship. In the fierce light of the history written by events during the next generation, hardly a line of his address failed to meet the test of truth and wisdom."

Webster, nevertheless, did not reach men's hearts as Clay had reached them. For too many years Webster had made a parade of his service to business. When he talked of the glory of the Union, his enemies had learned to compute the dividends the Union was paying to the Cotton Whigs of Massachusetts. In 1850 those dividends were high. Both maritime and manufacturing Massachusetts flourished on the Southern trade.

Year by year [writes Samuel Eliot Morison] the wealthy Cotton Belt wore out more boots and shoes, purchased more cottons for her slaves, used more Quincy granite in her public buildings, and consumed more Fresh Pond ice in her mint juleps. The New England mills, on their part, were calling for more cotton; and every pound of it that they received, before the Civil War, came by sailing vessel from Charleston, Savannah, Mobile, and New Orleans. The factory hands were equally hungry for cheap food. . . . In the period from September 1, 1841, to May 1, 1842, one-quarter of the lard, more than one-quarter of the flour, nearly half the pork and more than half the corn shipped out of New Orleans went to Boston.

Yankee ships also took cotton from New Orleans to Lancashire, Normandy, Flanders, Prussia, and the Baltic Provinces. Cotton, in fact, had become

the most important medium in our carrying trade, replacing colonial rum and codfish, and the Oriental goods of Federalist days. Few converts were obtained by the abolitionists in Boston counting-rooms. Society, business, and politics in Massachusetts were dominated by a triple entente between "the Lords of the Lash and the Lords of the Loom"—and the Lords of the Long Wharf.

In 1850, with the relatively low Walker Tariff and with hopes for a still lower tariff if the Democrats returned to power, this two-way trade profited the South as well as New England; but Southerners knew that Webster's ideal Union would be one in which Massachusetts sold her manufactures to the Cotton Kingdom at artificial high-tariff prices and bought her raw materials from the South at world prices. The South saw the threat of economic colonialism in Webster's Union; the Northern Free Soilers saw the shadow of State Street across Webster's noble sentiments. These suspicions do not diminish the splendor and the truth of the seventh of March speech; but they do explain why many good citizens refused to be moved by it.

Senator Seward of New York represented the younger generation of the North in the great debate. He spoke for the future: the ominous future, foreseen by Calhoun, wherein the South must choose abolition or secession. Seward spoke for the "Conscience Whigs," as opposed to the "Cotton Whigs"; he spoke for the Barnburners; he spoke for the men who were to form the Republican Party. He admitted that under the Constitution Congress could allow slavery in the territories "but there is a higher law than the Constitution which regulates our authority over the domain." "A higher law"—America was back again at her beginnings, back with Jefferson, and Locke, and Blackstone. "This law of nature . . . dictated by God himself . . . binding over all the globe . . . no human laws are of any validity, if contrary to this." It is hard to argue with people who know that their deeds correspond to the "higher law." And it is impossible to compromise with them.

Such certainty was not yet the mood of the majority, North or South. A number of influential Southerners, such as Alexander Stephens and Robert Toombs, were still in the Whig Party and worked loyally for the compromise. After months of debate the necessary measures passed in September, 1850. Calhoun had died meanwhile; and a Southern convention had met in Nashville to decide whether to take Calhoun's advice and demand special guarantees as the price of staying in the Union. Nine states were represented. South Carolina and Mississippi were for strong measures; but the majority chose moderation, and in the end the convention merely asked that the old Missouri Compromise line be extended to the Pacific.

It was fortunate for the Compromise that Zachary Taylor took his overdose of ice water while the debates were still in progress. He had come under the influence of Senator Seward, and he threatened to veto any agreement which did not contain the Wilmot Proviso. Clay protested that the President and his friends had declared "war, open war, undisguised war" against the Compromise. Fillmore, on the other hand, had said that in case of a tie vote in the Senate he would exercise his privilege as Vice-President and cast the deciding vote in favor of the Compromise. Once again, therefore, the death of a Whig President meant a reversal of Executive policy. On succeeding to office Fillmore at once changed the course of the debate by urging that Texas be paid ten million dollars for her boundary claim against New Mexico. Texas state securities, which were well distributed throughout the country, rose nine hundred per cent in value, and a new set of pressures was brought to bear on Congress. "The Texas Surrender Bill," wrote Senator Salmon P. Chase of Ohio, "was passed by the influence of the new administration which is Hunker and Compromise all over. The message of Fillmore . . . did the work."

Calhoun's predictions as to what would happen were so accurate that some have blamed him for the subsequent tragedy, as if he had brought it to pass by mentioning it. Others have felt

that the great Compromise was the culprit, and that Calhoun's proposal for a constitutional amendment should have been accepted. Yet this would only have aggravated what we have already seen to be a main problem of the American form of government: the problem of getting positive action in time. The government was devised to prevent action. With great difficulty and ingenuity (and with the able help of Marshall's Supreme Court and Jackson's advisers) it had cast off some of its chains, gained a little freedom and strength. Calhoun would have riveted the chains back on, and added a few more for safety. His "rule of the concurrent majority" meant that each major region, class, or economic interest must have a formal, constitutional right to veto action.

Like Jefferson and like most Americans of the early days Calhoun was certain that increased powers for the government meant decreased liberties for the people. Hence his fear of the Mexican War and of the doctrine of "manifest destiny"—of America's mission to spread liberty even by force. War kills liberty, said Calhoun. So does the rule of an unchecked majority. Liberty can only flourish when man is protected from the rulers of his own choice. The ruled, therefore, must be given "the means of making peaceable and effective resistance." And the one effective resistance is for each major interest and each section to have a veto. Obviously, if this were accepted, government would become impossible. Only in Jefferson's lost Arcadia could such a system work.

The nation was wise, therefore, to reject Calhoun's constitutional amendment. And it was also wise to adopt—extraconstitutionally, informally—many of Calhoun's proposals. The dilatory rule of the concurrent majority is a fair description of how, in normal times, the American party system operates. Out of the continent-wide welter of hopes and desires the parties build a compromise on which many diverse interests can agree. They do not ignore minorities, they incorporate and placate them. Each major party, in fact, is a league of minority groups—class, race, and regional. Such parties cannot afford to have hard and fast ideas, or to be Left, or Right, or even Middle. They must be all three at the same time, in different parts of the country. And they must make gentlemen's agreements (and committee rules) in Congress to prevent coalitions of enthusiasts from brushing aside minority protests. So, in truth, the party system provides for concurrent majorities, but in a subtler and more flexible form than Calhoun demanded.

Government by concurrent majority, however, would be death if it were written into the Constitution, for it must always break down at two points: it cannot act fast (so it must be overridden in an emergency), and it cannot deal with a conflict of principles. It can ward off unnecessary conflicts of principles. It can even pretend for a very long time that a conflict which clearly exists, and which cannot be dodged, does not exist at all—thus aggravating the problem deplorably. But it is a negative system, a system of inaction. And matters of principle, if they are so important that they must be settled, cannot be settled by inaction. This is what Jefferson feared, when he said that if the day came when a disagreement on moral principle was also a disagreement between sections the nation might fall.

THE LEGISLATIVE HISTORY OF THE COMPROMISE AND ITS IMMEDIATE AFTERMATH

George Fort Milton: STEPHEN A. DOUGLAS TAKES CHARGE

ON April 18 the Senate ordered and selected the Committee. The Chairman was Henry Clay. Lewis Cass gave added weight. Daniel S. Dickinson, of New York, had great prestige as an orator. Jesse D. Bright, of Indiana, was to represent the Democratic West. Daniel Webster, the leading member from New England, was offset by Phelps, a Vermont Free-Soiler. Cooper, of Pennsylvania, completed the Northern membership. In addition to Clay the South was represented by John Bell, of Tennessee, staunch Whig and advocate of Taylor's program; Berrien, of Georgia; Willie P. Mangum, of North Carolina, both doughty conservative Whigs; Mason, of Virginia, a disciple of Calhoun; King, of Alabama and Downs, of Louisiana. The group well reflected the variant sectional viewpoints represented in the Senate. But Douglas was not of the Thirteen.

There are various explanations for this omission. He had already impressed the Senate with his power, and his chairmanship of the Territorial Committee gave him a certain right of courtesy to membership upon the Select Committee. Some authorities have suggested that the omission marked a direct snub by Clay. But Douglas himself wrote Lanphier that he had been offered membership, but had "declined being a member," because he did not believe that the Omnibus Bill had any conceivable chance of

success and he wished to keep in a position to save something from the wreck.

Not in the least taken aback, the Little Giant requested that his California bill be considered immediately and that it be made the special order of the day. Henry Clay supported his request, but inasmuch as he was among the Senators selected to accompany Calhoun's remains to South Carolina, asked Douglas for an understanding that the bill would not be brought to a vote before the Committee returned. Douglas made it clear that his sole purpose was to expedite matters. When the bill was brought to the point of a test vote, he planned to defer it until the funeral committee returned. "That is exactly in conformity with the liberal, manly course of the Senator," Clay replied, serving notice that he intended to move to add Territorial and Texas boundary provisions to Douglas' California bill. On April 22 Cass remarked in debate that he thought it quite possible that the Thirteen would merely amend Douglas' measures.

In a fortnight the Thirteen's ideas changed, and on May 7 Clay told Douglas that the Committee would soon present an elaborate report but felt some embarrassment as to the bills. In their report, they would recommend that the Senate accept Douglas' California and Territorial bills and unite them into one act. Why did not Clay himself unite

George Fort Milton, *The Eve of Conflict* (Boston: Houghton Mifflin Company, 1934), pp. 67–78. Reprinted by permission.

these measures and have them reported as the Select Committee's bill? Douglas inquired. Clay answered that this would be neither just nor fair to Douglas, especially as the latter had done all the labor on them and had put them "in a form so perfect" that the Select Committee could not change them for the better in any point. In justice to Douglas they should be recommended to the Senate as they stood.

But the Little Giant insisted that he had no such pride in authorship as to desire that the Select Committee, out of regard to him, "should omit adopting that course which would . . . best accomplish the great object in view." Douglas reiterated his belief that, if the measures were united, they would unite the opponents of the measures, and therefore fail. If this were true, it would be better to have the Committee report them together, so that Douglas himself could renew them separately after a failure. Clay thanked him but repeated that it would be unjust.

"I respectfully ask you, Mr. Clay," Douglas countered, "what right have you, to whom the country looks for so much . . . to sacrifice to any extent the chances of success on a mere punctilio as to whom the credit may belong of having first written the bills? I, Sir, waive all claim and personal consideration in this matter, and insist that the Committee shall pursue the course . . . best calculated to accomplish the great end we all have in view." Clay was much touched. "You are the most generous man living," he exclaimed, stretching out his hand. "I will unite the bills and report them; but justice shall nevertheless be done you as the real author of the measures."

The next day the Committee of Thirteen presented its compromise. The main measures were a bill for admitting Cali-

fornia as a State and Utah and New Mexico as Territories; a provision for adjusting the Texas boundary dispute and a provision for abolishing the slave trade in the District of Columbia. A Fugitive Slave bill was already before the Senate and its passage was urged.

True to his word, Clay made it clear that the Committee's California bill was that reported by the Committee on Territories, and called attention to that body's "arduous and valuable labors." Indeed, the Select Committee's California bill literally consisted of copies of Douglas' two bills, joined together with a wafer. Only a single line had been added—a sentence prohibiting Territorial Legislatures from acting upon slavery. Douglas could quite truthfully boast to Lanphier that "the difference between Mr. Clay's compromise bill and my two bills was a wafer; he did not write one word of it, and I did write every word."

Douglas immediately sought a test as to whether the Senate preferred to consider the measures separately or in a single bill. After the Senate decided in favor of the latter plan he loyally supported its every item. But its course was troubled. President Taylor sneeringly termed it an "omnibus" and worked against it, while the Southern Ultras were no better pleased. On May 15 Jefferson Davis moved an amendent to prevent Territorial Legislatures from interfering "with those rights of property growing out of the institution of African slavery as it exists in any of the States of the Union." He modified his proposal a week later to assert that such legislatures should not pass any law "to introduce or exclude African slavery."

Douglas now sought to have the Senate eliminate the single new clause incorporated in the Committee's wafer joining his two bills. Expressing his regret "that a clause had been introduced into this bill providing that the Territorial Government should not legislate in respect to African slavery," he renewed his insistence that "this and all other questions relating to the domestic affairs and domestic policy of the Territories ought to be left to the decision of the people themselves." The inclusion of this new clause constituted "a violation of that principle upon which we have all rested our defense of the course we have taken on this question."

Davis responded that the difference between himself and Douglas was in their definition of a people. "The Senator says that the inhabitants of the Territory have a right to decide what their institutions shall be. When? By what authority? How many of them? The difference then between the Senator from Illinois and myself is the point at which the people do possess and may assert their rights."

Douglas took up the challenge. "If, Sir, there are enough to require a government," he replied, "and to authorize you to allow them to govern themselves, there are enough to govern themselves upon the subject of Negroes as well as concerning other species of property and other descriptions of institutions. You will concede that government is necessary—a government founded upon principles of Popular Sovereignty and the right of the people to enact their own laws. . . . You confer upon them the right to legislate upon all rightful subjects of legislation except Negroes. Why except the Negro? Why except African slavery? If the inhabitants are competent to govern themselves upon all other subjects . . . they are competent also to enact laws to govern themselves in regard to slavery and Negroes."

Soon afterwards Douglas moved to strike out the clause forbidding Territorial Legislatures to establish or prohibit "African slavery." The first effort was unsuccessful but a few days later the Senate accepted the change, and the bill was again in the exact form that Douglas had drafted it in March.

As the critical votes approached, the tension between President Taylor and the Compromise Whigs increased and the President exerted himself to the utmost to defeat the Compromise. Despondent, Clay wrote his son that "the Administration, the Ultra Southern men and the timid Whigs of the North" were all combined against it, and it would be "wonderful if it should succeed." Webster feared that the Administration was doomed, and the Whig party doomed with it. Cass, too, thought the Compromise doomed.

From the start the Southern course generated resentment. "We were actually goaded almost to madness," Shields wrote a friend back home. "They pounded on the North until it became insufferable." The Western members were exasperated by the bitterness of the extremists North and South. "The Ultra proslavery man is intolerable," Shields declared. "The Ultra Free-Soil man is still worse. It should be our effort to keep the middle course between two extremes. I am opposed to the extension of slavery. I believe Illinois opposed to it. But this opposition must be bounded by justice and moderation. There should be no 'Wilmot,' no attempt to interfere with the right of self-government in the Territories more than in the States. If the country keeps within the Constitution, they should be permitted to manage their own affairs. This is a sound principle but I am sorry to say it is not acceptable to the South."

While provoked over the way the Compromise debate caused Congress to neglect "the business affairs of the country," yet Douglas came to Clay's aid on nearly every issue that arose. When Berrien sought to delay the admission of California's Representatives into Congress, he defended their right to full and immediate representation. When Soulé, of Louisiana, sought to postpone California's admission until she had enacted an ordinance disclaiming all right to Federal public lands, Douglas spoke for two days in vigorous opposition. "It is admitted on all hands," Harris wrote, "the ablest speech Douglas ever delivered."

On July 4, following imprudent exposure at Washington Monument ceremonies, President Taylor was suddenly seized with cholera morbus and in a few days was at the point of death. On July 9 Webster rose during the usual acrimonious Senate debate to announce that the President was dying.

The death-bed scene was touching. The old General gasped for breath, and exclaimed: "I have endeavored to do my duty, I am prepared to die. My one regret is leaving behind me the friends I love." In a few minutes he was dead. Soon after the funeral Webster ran across his friend Hilliard, of Alabama, and they fell into discussion of the late President. "If General Taylor had lived," Webster said, "we should have had civil war."

Millard Fillmore's accession renewed Clay's hopes of passing the Compromise. The new President had long been a foe of Seward in New York politics, a fact which led him to become an advocate of Clay's Compromise. But these hopes proved illusory and Compromise hopes grew fainter and fainter. Jubilant, the Southern Ultras boasted that they would keep anything from being done; the Free-Soilers were equally pleased. Soon a great uproar would break out in the South, culminating in the much-threatened secession—such at least became the belief of Northern Democrats—and upon this, they felt sure, Free-Soilism, secretly pleased, would turn up pious eyes to say: "It is not my work—these villains always had treason in their hearts, and wanted only a pretext to commit the overt act."

In mid-July Harris had a long talk with Speaker Cobb. "He understands the movements of the South perfectly," the Illinois member noted, "and is fixed in the opinion that an open attempt at Secession will be made . . . Georgia, Alabama and Mississippi are not quite up to South Carolina, but so incessant is the conspirators' urging that they are fast bringing the masses to their views. Cobb is determined to be silent no longer." This altered attitude among such leaders of the Southern Whigs, reflected also by Stephens and Toombs, was later to have a powerful moderating effect both in Congress and in the States.

On July 17 Webster made his last Senate speech before accepting from Fillmore the Secretaryship of State. His swan-song was an elaborate appeal for the Compromise. He favored every measure of the Omnibus but thought that, whatever might be the fate of the Compromise as a whole, California should be immediately admitted. Did Douglas think the admission of California would settle the irksome question? he inquired.

"If California should be admitted by herself," the Illinois Senator answered, "I should certainly feel it my duty as Chairman of the Committee on Territories to move and take up the Territorial bills at once, and put them through, and also the Texas boundary question, and to settle them in detail if they are not settled in the aggregate."

"If this bill should fail today," Webster continued, "would you bring in that bill tomorrow?"

"Yes," was the laconic reply.

On July 25 Seward sought to have New Mexico admitted as a State, his speech evoking answering fury from the Southerners. Bradbury, of Maine, wanted the Texas line fixed by a joint commission of Texas and the United States, but would not have the new boundary operative until Texas had accepted it. All knew Texas would never do so and this scheme too was voted down.

By July 31 the whole matter was in such a tangle that motion was made that action on the Omnibus bill be indefinitely postponed. Marshaling his forces to oppose this, Clay was momentarily successful but the victory was short-lived. A few minutes later the New Mexican Territorial provision was eliminated. Next the Texas boundary provision was stricken from the bill. Then three attempts were made to eliminate the California bill, the final one successfully. Nothing was now left of the Omnibus except the establishment of a Territorial Government for Utah. The mountain had labored and had brought forth a mouse.

The defeat of the Omnibus marked the departure of all of the great triumvirate from the senatorial stage. Calhoun had been the first to go. Four months before, as if he despaired of securing from fleshly hands that perfect equilibrium for which he pleaded, his frail body had been consigned to the grave, and his weird logic willed to his lieutenants—a legacy destined to be paid in blood. Webster, too, had left his favorite forum. No more would the idle loiterers start up on seeing him approach in the uniform of the Revolution. He had had his last "great day," and now was again enjoying the comfortable office and pleasing dignity of Secretary of State. Clay was still a member of the Senate, but despondent, disillusioned and worn. He had poured all his energy and hope into the ill-fated Omnibus, it had failed, and the future seemed "dark and portentous."

On August 1 he rebuked the Senate for its course. "We presented to the country a measure of peace, a measure of tranquillity," he declared, "one which would have harmonized all the discordant feelings which prevailed. . . . The measure was defeated by the extremists on the other side of the Chamber, and on this." He stood in his place, he continued defiantly, "meaning to be unawed by any threats, whether they came from individuals, or from States." Furthermore, "if any one State, or a portion of the people of any State, choose to place themselves in military array against the Government of the Union, I am for trying the strength of the Government." It was time to find out "whether we have got a Government or not."

His final salvo against disunion was that not his State but the Union was his country. "Even if it were my own State," he shouted, "if my own State, lawlessly, contrary to her duty, should raise the standard of disunion against the residue of the Union, I would go against her. I would go against Kentucky herself in that contingency, much as I love her." Soon afterwards he left for Newport to repair his health in the refreshing breezes of the New England coast.

On that same day Douglas took charge of the abandoned Compromise. During all the debates Clay's plan had received his "active and unwavering support." His Illinois colleague, General Shields, had gone with him, as had all but two of the State's delegation in the House. From the start, Douglas had predicted that Clay would fail because it would unite the enemies of the various items. Harris believed that the Compromise had been "dashed to pieces by the carelessness or over-carefulness of its friends," but the Little Giant ascribed the defeat to "a union between the Free-Soilers and Disunionists and the Administration of Gen'l Taylor." To accomplish it, "all the power and patronage of the Gov't. was brought to bear against us, and at last the allied forces were able to beat us." Analyzing the votes upon the Compromise, he saw how the juncture of the measures had "united the opponents of each measure, instead of securing the friends of each." Similarly he saw how resolving the Omnibus bill into its individual components would enable him to secure the passage of each in turn.

More than this, the Little Giant sensed the changing temper of the country. The much-advertised Nashville Convention had been expected to prove that the great mass of the Southern people were ready to break up the Union. When the delegates assembled, their Ultra and unrepresentative character was clearly apparent and the real strength of the Southern Unionists began to be revealed.

In the North, too, sentiment began to change. Developments in Illinois were indicative. Many of the Free-Soil Whig leaders, in and out of the State Legislature, who had been insisting on a Wilmot prohibition, saw the situation in a new light and came out for compromise. The Illinois Democrats in Congress were overjoyed at these developments. "Now, by Saint Paul, the work goes bravely on!" Harris chortled. He believed a Whig schism had occurred, and that "those profligate politicians, who have driven the country to the verge of dissolution were becoming conscious of their errors, and were seeking to save themselves from the consequences of their acts."

These shifts in public opinion North and South aided Douglas in his new task. He amended the caption of the ill-fated Omnibus so as to make it accurately descriptive of the Utah Territorial establishment. This done, he promptly reintroduced the bill for the admission of California as a State and asked that it be so amended as to reinstate a public land provision earlier stricken out. The Senate heeded Douglas' request and put the clause back in. Two hostile amendments were then offered, the first to divide the State into two parts, on a parallel of 35° 30′, the second to divide it on the parallel of 36° 30′. He opposed both.

He was immediately charged with inconsistency in opposing the extension of the Missouri Compromise line to the Pacific Coast. For three months he had been silent under similar attack. Now he undertook to meet it. He admitted that in 1848 he had offered a similar amendment to the Oregon bill. "I was then willing to adjust this whole slavery question on that line and on those terms," he said. "If the whole acquired territory was now in the same condition as it was then, I would vote for it, should be glad to see it adopted. But since then California has increased in population, has a State Government organized, and I cannot consent, for one, to destroy that State Government. . . . For that reason, and that alone, I shall vote against the amendment." Then he forced the two proposals to a vote and was able to have both rejected.

At this period Douglas seemed quite concerned to prove his own consistency. He caused the *Illinois State Register* to answer the charge that he was a slaveowner, and to correct the charge that he was a Free-Soiler. As the Springfield editor explained, under instructions, the Senator had opposed the Wilmot Proviso, had "always advocated the right of the people in each State and Territory to decide the slavery question for themselves," and only voted for the prohibition of slavery in 1850's Territorial bills in obedience to instructions: "The vote was the vote of those who gave the instructions and not his own." A little later, Douglas asked again that the paper make it plain that any vote which he had given or would give, seemingly inconsistent to that principle, was not his vote but "the vote of those who gave the instructions."

Henry Clay had sought to float the Compromise to success upon a sea of stately speeches. During the five months from February to August he had been on hand every day the Senate was in session, had made several set speeches and had addressed the Senate more than seventy times. Indeed, so great were his oratorical exertions that, by the time of the defeat of the Compromise, his health had completely broken down.

With Douglas' accession to command there came a distinct shift in strategy. A past-master of parliamentary procedure, the Little Giant had an uncanny knowledge of the various combinations he could devise to sustain the diverse items of his program. Already "some of the chivalry," alarmed at the result of their conduct, had begun to back down. Well aware of the situation, and secure in his leadership, Douglas let others stalk the boards while he directed the stage.

The Senate responded readily to the new management. After his third day in command Douglas felt so confident of success that he wrote Lanphier sanguinely: "We have the greatest confidence that we will yet be able to settle the whole difficulty before we adjourn."

He then revealed his plans for the various items of the Compromise. The Senate was at the moment engaged on his California bill. "I trust you will hear of its passage through the Senate before you receive this. We shall then take up a bill for the Texas boundary which Mr. Pearce of Maryland and myself are now preparing. . . . We shall then take up the bill for New Mexico and pass it just as I reported it four months ago. Thus will all bills pass the Senate, and I believe the House also. When they are all passed, you see they will be collectively Mr. Clay's Compromise, and separately the bills reported by the Committee on Territories four months ago."

So far as earlier efforts had been concerned, Douglas felt that "if Mr. Clay's name had not been associated with the bills, they would have passed long ago. The Administration were jealous of him and hated him and some Democrats were weak enough to fear that the success of his bill would make him President. But let it always be said of Old Hal that he fought a glorious and patriotic battle. No man was ever governed by higher and purer motives."

In accordance with Douglas' plan, on August 5 Pearce introduced his bill for the settlement of the northern boundary of Texas. During the ensuing four days' debate, except to answer questions, Douglas spoke only once. This speech was to assure the Senate that any change made in this bill would automatically be incorporated in the New Mexico bill when that measure came forward. On August 9 the bill passed by a vote of 30 to 20.

Three days later Douglas spoke at some length upon the main measure.

Answering attacks on the irregularity of the California constitutional procedure, he offered the illustration of Michigan. His advocacy was both compelling and successful, for the bill passed the Senate the next day and another item of Douglas' original measures was enacted practically in the form of its initial draft.

The Little Giant at once called up his New Mexico bill, and moved to strike out all sections in it referring to the government of Utah and the solution of the Texas boundary. This was promptly done. Enemies of the measure then brought forward amendment after amendment, but each was defeated. The Illinois leader then brought the bill to a vote and it passed. Then he moved to change the title of the measure so as to omit the name of Utah—a small matter, but quickly voted, another illustration of his effective leadership.

Thus, under Douglas' leadership, in two weeks' time, the Senate had voted to admit California, to quiet the Texas boundary dispute and to give New Mexico Territorial Government. The Little Giant had proved his mastery.

But the passage of the measures through the Senate was only half of the battle. As late as June, Douglas' House associates had felt certain of their ability to pass the Compromise. In August, however, when the Senate bills started coming over, defeat stared the House managers in the face. The Senator gave the closest attention to the House progress of the various bills. He had great personal influence and prestige there, exercised it to the fullest and his leadership proved effective.

The danger in the House was the same that had been met in the Senate. Southern Ultras and Northern Free-Soilers, equally unwilling to yield to the idea of compromise, were not unwilling to join hands to negative a middle course. Of the two, the anger of the Southerners seemed the more intense, but the great strength of Wilmot Whigs made their attitude politically more dangerous.

By the last of August it seemed that the Texas boundary bill was sure to be killed in the House. The Northwestern Democrats were mainly for it but the Whigs were acting badly. "No sooner do they see a prospect of settlement than they want to make the most they can of party capital out of it," Harris wrote bitterly to Lanphier. "Some of them now want simply to pass the California bill and the boundary bill and to relieve the Administration of the troubles, and let the Territorial bills go." The plan of the Northern enemies of the Compromise—chiefly Whigs still anxious to carry out the Taylor scheme of six months before—was to pass a Texas boundary bill, admit California as a State, and do nothing further about the other elements of the Compromise.

To counter this scheme, Linn Boyd, of the House Committee on Territories, had Douglas prepare a literal copy of the Senate's New Mexican bill so that it could be offered as an amendment to the Texas boundary bill. Douglas did so. Boyd introduced the amendment, the Free-Soilers saw their danger and factional turmoil broke out.

On September 1 the struggle began in earnest. Loyally following Douglas' lead and constantly advised by him, the Western Democrats undertook to carry through the Compromise as a whole. All that was needed, Harris believed, was for the Territorial bill to pass; that done, the road lay open for full adjustment.

When Boyd's amendment was brought to a vote, the Northern Whigs turned against it, and it was 46 votes short of passage. On September 4, when the Texas boundary bill, shorn of Boyd's amendment, was brought up again, enough of the Northern Whigs turned away to defeat it. "Nothing can effect a settlement," Harris indignantly wrote, "until Whiggery caves in, admits its follies and its political wickedness, and strangles its Proviso bantling." They knew they could pass the bill with Boyd's amendment, he added a little later, "yet the cowardly tricksters voted against that amendment because it had not the Wilmot in it. They wanted it passed, and they would then have voted for the bill in numbers sufficient to have carried it. But they were committed, as they say, against Territorial Governments unless the Proviso was on."

But the disappointment was shortlived. The Compromise leaders saw that the defeat was solely technical and parliamentary and that, "Lazarus-like," the bills would come forth from the grave and be passed. The day after the adverse vote Douglas wrote confidently that the bill would come to life. Cobb stayed in the Speaker's chair "during two days of the most exciting scenes I have ever witnessed."

Early on the afternoon of September 6, these maneuvers had their effect, and Harris was able to address a joyous note to Douglas: "Boundary bill and New Mexico bill just ordered to 1 reading by ten maj. All danger is over—all's bright, and everybody but the Abolitionists or disunionists glad. The sneaking, contemptible Whig pups of the North barked *No* at the bill all through, with a few venerable exceptions. . . . Glory to God in the highest."

Among spectators of this triumph were Lewis Cass and Henry Clay. The latter, who had returned from Newport on August 28, was only moderately pleased at Douglas' success. "We can see no end yet of this fatiguing session," he wrote his son soon thereafter. "I am again getting very much exhausted. I wish that I had remained longer at Newport."

Clay had returned in time to take part in the debate on the two remaining items of the Compromise—the abolition of the slave trade in the District of Columbia and the enactment of a better Fugitive Slave law. During the debate on the first of these, Seward proposed to abolish slavery itself in the District, a motion which occasioned lurid fireworks but was rejected with only five affirmative votes. After two weeks' general debate, the Senate passed the original measure by 33 to 19.

The other item of the program, a new Fugitive Slave bill, was also enacted into law. Originally fashioned by Mason, of Virginia, it was an integral part of the Compromise and had the general assent of the moderates. But while Douglas favored it, he was not on hand to vote, a circumstance which laid him open to the charge that he had tried to dodge.

Always adventurous in land speculations, Douglas' obligations were constantly maturing. In September, 1850, his note for $4000 was about to fall due in New York. He thought that he had made arrangements to meet it, but these fell through and he rushed to the metropolis.

Before he left, several Senators assured him that debate over the Fugitive Slave bill would continue for at least another week. But the Senate acted with unusual promptness. On Douglas' second evening in New York, while he was dining with some friends from Illinois, he was surprised to learn that the bill had already been ordered engrossed for its third and final reading. He left immediately for Washington but arrived after the vote had been taken and the bill had gone over to the House.

The Little Giant wished to explain the reasons for his failure to vote but Shields held him back. Everyone knew that Douglas favored the bill, the General said. Also, in all likelihood, it would come back from the House with amendments and Douglas would then get a chance to vote. The charge that he had sought to escape passing on this bill seemed absurd to Douglas, and appears equally absurd to the modern historical student. As he said later, "Dodging votes, an attempt to avoid responsibility, is no part of my system of political tactics."

Finally these two measures likewise passed the House, and by the end of September every item which Douglas deemed necessary for the solution of the sectional difficulties had become law. Convinced that the sectional disputes had been completely quieted, he "resolved never to make another speech upon the slavery question in the Houses of Congress."

During the latter part of his labors for the Compromise, its new general had to contend against sickness as well as Abolitionists and Southern Ultras. For much of September he was crippled, "and kept in constant torture by a very painful and deep-seated swelling on his hip." But, painful as this was, Douglas stayed at his task until the session ended.

Nor was his agency in the success of the Compromise without notice. "If any man has a right to be proud of the success of these measures," Jefferson Davis, of Mississippi, an opponent of the Compromise, declared in the final debate, "it is the Senator from Illinois." Clay proclaimed the final success of the program as "a triumph for the Union, for harmony and concord" and added that "to Douglas, more than to any other individual," was due the fact that disruption had been averted. Douglas declared himself proud of having played "an humble part in the enactment of all these great measures," but said firmly that "no man and no party has acquired a triumph except the party friendly to the Union."

In essence, he felt that the great principle of the Compromise was its endorsement of "the right of the people to form and regulate their own internal concerns and domestic institutions in their own way." A large group of Southern Compromise men were equally delighted with the outcome. They too felt that a great essential principle had been secured. But they saw the new principle not a national but a sectional one. Robert Toombs was again and again to proclaim that the Compromise upheld "the principle of non-interference with slavery by Congress, the right of the people to hold slaves in a common Territory."

The discrepancy between these views of the basis of the Compromise was fundamental. Under Douglas' view, if they so determined, the people of the Territory could exclude slavery. Did Toombs and the other Southern Compromisers understand the measures of 1850 to embrace this right?

Here was a portent of further disagreement between the sections. The Missouri Compromise had failed to still the clash of sections and it had been necessary to abandon it. Perhaps this new Compromise contained within itself further seeds of strife. Would the new statesmanship prove equal to the task of continual adjustment? Upon this depended the Nation's peace.

Allan Nevins: ACQUIESCENCE WITH CONDITIONS
AND RESERVATIONS

PEACE, prosperity, and Union—all over the South these seemed to be the watchwords of the new era. There had never been any question that the border area, including North Carolina, and the Southwest, full of pioneer nationalism, strongly approved the Compromise. The two old cotton States of South Carolina and Georgia, and the two new cotton States of Alabama and Mississippi, had been the danger points; and even they had uttered a decisive "No." Strong pressure came from national Democratic leaders for reknitting the party fabric and dropping the disunionist clamor. They feared that unless the Rhetts and Quitmans subsided, a permanent Union Party would take root in the South, sorely injuring or even destroying the Democratic organization. Douglas and Buchanan were insistent, in their letters to Southern Democrats, that the quarrel must cease, and they were backed by the Washington *Union*, which this year passed under the editorship of Andrew Jackson Donelson, Jackson's oldtime protégé and secretary. In fact, a cohort of Democratic leaders in the North now insisted that the Rhetts and Yanceys keep still; that Howell Cobb and Foote, the chief beneficiaries of the Union Party, return to the regular fold; and that all should rally about the old party tenets.

In retrospect, three main factors could be seen as responsible (beyond a basic love of the Union) for the utter rout of secessionist forces in the cotton States. The first was the general flush of prosperity throughout the region. This prosperity, remarked the *Spirit of the South*, explained the reluctance to undertake resistance; "because there is plenty to live on, because we are out of debt, and cotton brings a good price, many are in so good a humor and so well satisfied with themselves and things around them as to shut their eyes to the future in the consoling reflection that the future cannot hurt them." Men would not fly from affluence to ills they knew not of; ills vividly pictured by the Alabama *Journal*. "Disunion will not give us a better price for cotton—will not increase the value of slave property—will not render them more secure—will not diminish taxation— but will be likely under the best imaginable state of affairs to double taxation, diminish the price of our staples, and reduce the value of negroes and land, fifty per cent." B. F. Perry later stated his conviction that many wealthy South Carolinians who ostensibly backed the secession ticket were delighted by its defeat. He had heard a friend say that the wealthiest rice-planter of the State, who voted for disunion, would at any time have given privately his draft for $100,-000 to crush it.

Along with economic factors, the political situation operated against secession in 1850–51. In Alabama and Georgia, as in North Carolina, Tennessee, and other States, the Whigs were still powerful—still nearly equal to the Democrats. Both parties were badly divided on the question. In any clear-cut contest the Unionist majority of the Whigs could unite with the Unionist minority of the Democrats to carry the day; and in some areas it could unite with a Unionist Democratic majority! Not until the Whig party was destroyed, permitting a group of secessionists in key States to capture the single party of strength and use its machinery, would revolutionary action be feasible. It might be added that not until the differences between separatist secessionists and coöperative secessionists were erased would such capture be easy.

✓ Finally, the social and cultural development of the South as a separate entity was still much too immature to let secessionist tendencies attain vigorous growth. The rise of separate Southern churches, the diffusion of newspapers and magazines preaching an aggressive Southernism, the use of Southern textbooks in the schools, the Southern commercial conventions, Southern poetry and fiction, and above all Southern polemics, were bringing into existence a national spirit; but that is always a plant of slow growth. In 1850, hundreds of thousands who ten years later would think of themselves as Southerners still thought of themselves simply as Americans.

It was significant of the importance of economic factors that Unionist leaders sounded a clarion call for more attention to internal development and less waste of energy on national dissension. The neglect of urgent improvements, said Perry in his *Southern Patriot*, was driving thousands of citizens from South Carolina. Let her extend her railroads and plank roads, build up her manufactories, erect public buildings like the new Statehouses of Tennessee and North Carolina, begin furnishing her own iron, granite, and marble, and above all, develop her schools, academies, and colleges. Let her encourage the direct import and export of merchandise and products. The same cry was raised in Alabama and Mississippi. One of the principal exponents of economic development in Alabama was Daniel Pratt, successful manufacturer of textiles and gins in Autauga County. Saying that incendiary speeches about secession were silly while the State's industries were so primitive, he exhorted Alabamians to go quietly to work to provide their own coal, iron, hardware, farm-implements, clothing, and shoes. Expounding his doctrines in the Alabama *Journal,* he hailed the abolitionist agitation as a much-needed alarm bell to awaken the South to industrial activity. The Alabama legislature in the session of 1851–52 chartered two companies for direct trade between Mobile and Europe, and subsidized them by exempting the sale of direct imports from taxes.

In the political field, strenuous efforts were made during the winter of 1851–52 to reorganize and reknit the Democratic Party. With the Presidential election of 1852 looming ahead, unity was imperative. In Alabama the ranks were almost fully closed. Yancey, temporarily putting on the garb of meekness, made speeches advising the people to accept the Georgia platform. Only the sternest Unionists of north Alabama and the wildest secessionists of her rich Black Belt refused to clasp hands. In Mississippi also most of the discordant elements fell into line. Foote, arriving in Jackson on a chill January day for his inauguration, was greeted by cannon, banners, and the jubilant yells of a surging crowd. In his inaugural address he congratulated the country on the fact that the Compromise had commanded the hearty approval of nineteen-twentieths of the American people, saying that in Mississippi not a single voice was now heard in opposition to a series of measures which six months before were assailed by thousands with language of bitter denunciation and caustic ridicule.

In Georgia greater trouble was encountered. "Seeing that the State would be chained to the Car of Whiggery for all future time unless the Democratic party could be reorganized and restored to vigor," Herschel V. Johnson later explained to Franklin Pierce, "a meeting of such Democrats as could be got together was held on the 13th of November, 1851, in Milledgeville, during the session of the legislature, to adopt measures for that purpose. That meeting appointed a committee . . . to report to a subsequent meeting to be held at the capital on the evening of the 25th of November. . . . I hand you a copy of the report and proceedings of that meeting, that you may see for yourself how *formally* and how distinctly, we abandoned the Southern Rights organization and unfurled the old Democratic Banner. I beg you to read it, as a matter of justice to the Democratic party of Georgia. Does it not breathe the right spirit? Does it contain a word that ought to offend our Union *Democratic* brethren? Would it not seem, to any candid mind, that it ought to have resulted in the entire harmony of the party? So far from this, I assure you, not a single Union Democrat united in the meeting; but the whole Union press was out in full cry against us, denouncing us as 'hypocrites,' 'secessionists,' 'fire-eaters,' 'disunionists,' etc., etc." Yet even in Georgia ultimate reconciliation took place on the "Georgia Platform."

It was the Whig Party which in the end suffered most heavily from the strains of the Compromise. It, too, underwent a process of reorganization in the cotton belt. But the Alabama editor who stated that the election of 1851 had killed the Whig Party dead as a mackerel in his State, and that by the fall of 1852 a Whig there would be a curiosity, hit near the truth. The main reasons were three, and were obvious to all. First, the tendency of the Northern Whigs to attack Southern institutions made it difficult to remain allied with them without incurring discredit. Second, the Whig Party had lost its chief principles; tariff protection and internal improvements too definitely favored the North to have any appeal to the South. Third, the impending deaths of Clay and Webster would remove the only two Whig leaders of truly national prestige. While the path of the Democratic Party in the South was thorny enough, that of the Whig Party turned definitely downward to obliteration.

Acquiescence had triumphed in the South. But this fatal weakness of the Whig Party was one reason for regarding the future with misgiving. Another ground for apprehension lay in continued recalcitrancy of a bold band of leaders. Yancey continued to watch, wait, and intrigue. One of the organs of his clan, the Dallas, Ala., *Gazette*, said in the fall of 1851 that it was immovable: "For our part when we hoisted the banner of Southern Rights at our masthead, we did so with a determination to stand by it through weal or woe; and come what may, we shall not strike it until the South is independent, or her people sunk so low in the sea of submission as to be forever beyond the hope of resurrection." Rhett closed the year 1851 with a speech saying that he had been a disunionist since 1841, and was a disunionist still. His reasons boiled down to a conviction that the South was steadily being overbalanced and overwhelmed, and that she was being unjustly treated in the distribution of territory. He would fight to the end, he said, to keep his section from being made another Hungary.

But above all, it had to be remembered that Southern acquiescence was conditional. The Georgia Platform was a sufficiently clear warning, and it was underlined in the summer of 1851 by the action of the Mississippi Union Convention in appending to strongly pacific resolutions the emphatic addendum: "Resolved, that it is our deliberate opinion, that upon the faithful execution of the Fugitive Slave law, by the proper authorities, depends the preservation of our much-loved Union."

*   *   *

The moral impulse which helped rear the anti-slavery movement was of course most deeply touched when a fleeing Negro carried into a Northern community the spectacle of his helplessness, his wrongs, and his anguish. The very act of running away commonly argued moral or physical maltreatment and a poignant desperation. Few black men and women faced the hardships of a long and lonely flight, the perils of pursuit, recapture, and punishment, the uncertainties of freedom in an alien land, without heartache and dark misgiving. They began their hazardous journey, usually without a penny, a friend, or a bit of property save the poor clothes on their backs, because they had no decent choice: because their families had been broken up by sale, because they were brutally punished, or because they were threatened with transportation "down the river" to the sugar and cotton fields of the Lower South. And when they crossed the Ohio or Delaware, were the free communities they entered to yield them up to professional slave-catchers, furious in pursuit

of their quarry? The great majority of Northerners in 1850 had no desire to interfere with slavery where it existed; possibly a majority would still permit it some little extension. But this same majority would die in its tracks before it would aid the slaveholder to hunt down his harried, panting, wild-eyed bondsman.

Hence it was that the passage of the new Fugitive Slave Act sent a wave of defiant indignation across the North, mitigated only by a strong conviction that it could never be enforced. On this point the demand for conformity stuck in the throats of even the mildest. The conservative Robert C. Winthrop, praising Fillmore's annual message at the close of 1850, wrote that he should not have emphasized so much the word *final*, "as if the Fugitive Slave law was to be as unchangeable as the laws of the Medes and the Persians—which, by the bye, it more resembles in some of its details than any American or European code." Everett agreed. He had already declared that he would never obey the act. "I admit the right of the South to an efficient extradition law; but it is a right *that cannot be enforced*. The difficulty with the old law was that it was against the feeling of the people." Writing to Webster, he had pointed out a certain inconsistency on the part of Southerners. Senator Butler had defended the Charlestonians who in 1846 drove Rockwood Hoar from their city, on the ground that if he had remained he would have been mobbed; but Hoar had gone there merely to argue in the circuit court the second section of the fourth article of the Constitution—the same section which grants the right of extradition. "If such a cause is enough to rouse a mob in Charleston, how can Southern gentlemen expect our mob to assist in arresting their fugitive?"

It was true that the South expected a more precise observance of the Constitution in the North than it was ready to furnish at home. Any Northerner who travelled below the Potomac to announce a lecture on slavery would have been in peril, and any man who scattered an anti-slavery pamphlet in a Southern town would have been lucky to escape with summary ejectment. When black cooks and stewards entered certain Southern ports they were temporarily locked up, though their presence offered no real danger. The excuse of the Southerners for unconstitutional interferences with freedom of speech, the press, the mails, and the person was the state of public excitement and the danger of slave insurrection. Within limits it was a valid excuse; but the South was unwilling to extend to Northern sentiment the same tolerance.

Tolerance was particularly needed because the provisions of the new law were excessively harsh and stringent. Southerners would have been wise if, at the cost of losing a few more slaves, they had satisfied themselves with a milder enactment. The main complaints of the Northern people were four. First, the act allowed no jury trial for fugitives, though the Constitution provided that in suits at common law where the value in controversy exceeded twenty dollars jury trial should be maintained. The claimant's affidavit established his title. Second, the act did not allow the fugitive even a hearing before a judge, but authorized the captor to take him at once before a Federal commissioner, specially attached to the usual courts by the new law, who was empowered to issue a certificate for hurrying the Negro off to slavery without stay or appeal. Third, the commissioner was to get ten dollars if he directed the return of the captive, but only five if he ordered a release. The reason given was that the papers for a return involved more labor, but Northerners were quick to assert that the extra payment was in effect a bribe. Anson Burlingame remarked that the law fixed the price of a Carolina Negro at one thousand dollars, and of a Yankee soul at five! Finally, the marshal or deputies charged with the arrest of the alleged fugitive were subject to a fine of $1,000 if they refused to execute it; they were empowered to summon all citizens to their aid; and any person who concealed or rescued a fugitive might be fined $1,000, imprisoned for six months, and mulcted $1,000 in civil damages for every slave so lost—all this seeming excessively severe.

These four complaints were iterated and reiterated by the North. What chiefly distressed calm-minded people was the possibility that a Negro who had lived for years in a Northern community, industrious and useful, might now be rapt from home and friends to lifelong servitude on flimsy evidence presented in *ex parte* fashion to a prejudiced Federal placeholder.

It was unfortunate that in a group of laws adopted with conciliatory intent, one should so bristle with offence to a multitude of patriotic Americans. Originally the measure had provided for jury trial. That is, the committee of thirteen had reported a bill which required that the owner or agent reclaiming an alleged fugitive should take him home, bring him before the first court meeting there, and if he asserted his freedom, submit the case to twelve sworn men. This was satisfactory, for as the committee stated, colored persons suing for freedom usually found attorneys quick to defend them, and met with general sympathy. But in the final bill this provision for jury trial was stricken out.

All well-informed people knew that the fifth amendment to the Constitution, stipulating that no person should be deprived of life, liberty, or property without due process of law, and the seventh, safeguarding the right of jury trial, had been carried in response to an overwhelming public demand, and that for centuries the right of jury trial had been one of the proudest of Anglo-American traditions. John Van Buren declared the Fugitive Slave Act flagrantly unconstitutional. On this point the best authorities were against him. But Lincoln was quite right in saying later that the law should have been so framed that a free Negro would be in no greater danger of slavery under it than an innocent man would be of hanging under the murder laws. The deletion of the jury clause saved a few slaves annually to the South at the cost of alienating countless thousands of former friends of the section.

Theodore Parker had declared that slavery was ringed about by a contracting wall of flame. The harsh character of the new law cast oil upon the circle of fire. While it was pending the religious journals of the North with remarkable unanimity either condemned it outright, or asserted that no humane man could help enforce it. The New York *Evangelist* said that no human compact could bind the conscience of the people to such revolting work as helping recapture slaves. The New York *Independent* asserted that "the slave catcher shall not budge an inch further than he now does in the North"—that every village would spurn him. The New York *Observer* believed there was "no respectable man, whose feelings would not revolt at the thought of aiding in the capture of fugitive slaves," while the Boston *Christian Register* was for treating the Constitution in this matter as a dead letter. *Zion's Herald*, a Methodist organ, predicted that if Webster compelled men to the odious work of slave catching, the curses of his fellow-citizens would follow him through life and those of their children would fall upon his grave. The Boston *Watchman and Reporter,* the leading Baptist journal, avowed that "even with the alternative of disunion" the North could "sanction no concession." Theocracy was dead in America, but religious interventionism in politics was still powerful.

When morality enters public affairs the general principle has a thunderous voice, and in both morals and economics fear of evils to come is a far greater excitant than any immediate loss. These facts explain why, under the heat generated by the Fugitive Slave Act, mustard seeds sprang everywhere into trees. Had both North and South sat down quietly, appraised the number and value of the fugitive slaves, got at the truth about all reports of the kidnapping of free Negroes, and refrained from emotion and exaggeration, agreement might have been possible. Both sides were equally guilty of hysteria. As Clay pointed out, while his border State of Kentucky, which was most exposed to loss, showed little irritation, the Deep South, from which flight was extremely difficult, lashed itself into fury. No precise figures of the number of fugitives are available. But according to the Census of 1850, only sixteen out of almost 400,-000 South Carolina slaves ran away that year. According to estimates embodied in the Census of 1860, the year 1850 saw only about a thousand slaves running away; most of them came from the border area; and by no means all of them got into free States. It was notorious that in Maryland and Delaware many slaveholders thought themselves well rid of runaways, and that many slaves were manumitted to save the trouble of holding them. But many Southerners, relying on wild guesses, convinced themselves that a hundred thousand Negroes had escaped, and that the losses ran into tens of millions—the relatively safe Cotton States showing the greatest anger!

Parts of the North, though on the whole small parts, were equally unreasonable. Pursuit and recapture would naturally be commonest along the border, yet it was far-off New England, Michigan, and Wisconsin which evinced the most fury. Webster in 1850 diligently inquired among New England Congressmen as to cases of seizure. He found that (so far as this source of information went) no alleged fugitive slave had ever been seized by a lawful master in Maine; none had ever been seized in New Hampshire; none had ever been seized in Vermont; none had been seized in Rhode Island within the past twenty years; and only one had been seized in Connecticut—that case, some twenty-five years earlier, having terminated in the immediate discharge of the Negro for want of identification. Several seizures had taken place in Massachusetts, but the history of only one was known; that, a capture in Boston in the late 1830's, having ended when the owner accepted a sum which he regarded as less than half the value of the fugitive. Yet many New Englanders talked as if their section was certain to be filled with lawless slavecatchers. While Southerners complained that an honest planter, trying to recover property to which his constitutional title was clear, would be in danger of criminal prosecution for kidnapping, suits for false imprisonment, and even "of being mobbed or being put to death in a street fight by insane fanatics or brutal ruffians," some Northerners cried that brutal gangs of manhunters, running down free Negroes, would compel assistance under penalty of fine, imprisonment, and heavy civil damages.

All explorers of the sociology of agitation will recognize that this situation was ideal for fomenting disorder and strife. In conditions of great public tension the indirect effect of statutes is far greater than their direct results. The Fugitive Slave Act did not accomplish much in the recapture of slaves—though numerous recaptures, and alas! some illegal kidnappings, did take place. But it effected wonders in the stimulation of pro-slavery agitation. Feeling for and against the law ran so high that every instance of opposition was dramatized as on a floodlighted stage; every defiance to it resounded as through a megaphone. Senator Mason was given a banquet in Warrenton, Va., to celebrate his victory in writing and passing the law. But had he and such Northern friends as Buchanan, who grew violent in asserting that it was "the only measure of the Compromise calculated to secure the rights of the South," been trying to play into the hands of propagandists and troublemakers, they could have taken no more efficient step. Part of the drive to make the law so drastic had unquestionably come from men who, like Jefferson Davis, wanted to defeat the Compromise, and failing in that, to keep agitation alive.

ETHICS AND POLITICS

Dorothy Fosdick: ETHICAL STANDARDS
AND POLITICAL STRATEGIES

A DANGEROUS assumption about the nature of morality lies at the root of the more disastrous political strategies of our time. To assume the existence of an absolute ethic, to interpret right behavior as conformity to unconditional rules of good conduct has serious results. St. Francis of Assisi maintained that men are under the absolute command of God to love their neighbors as themselves. Machiavelli believed that if a prince did not remain faithful to a priori prescriptions of good behavior he was acting contrary to morality; no matter what the practical results, if he lied, or killed, or stole he was doing wrong. Kant argued that morality consists in obedience to a categorical imperative of duty. Whenever rules of conduct are thus believed to be right or wrong in themselves without reference to their social consequences, an absolute ethic is assumed.

There are today two types of men who presuppose such an ethic, and thereby tend to disqualify themselves for making political decisions. On the one hand, there is the man who is confident that categorical rules of right behavior can be followed and so insists on literal obedience to them. On the other hand, there is the man who is convinced that such rules cannot be followed, and so advocates that they be ignored.

To the first class belong our modern monks, and what Alfred Zimmern happily calls our "part-time monks." These men want to live strictly according to an absolute ethic. They intend to love their neighbors "with a passionate literalness of approach." They do not propose to lie, or to kill, or to steal. Indeed in their eyes moral rules must be respected regardless of the cost either to themselves or to society. The monks, unwilling to make any compromise with the prudential ethic of the world, draw apart into a simpler sphere of their own, living in isolated communities where they can find their neighbors and be of service to them, or joining monastic groups where they have no wife or child of their own to monopolize their love. The part-time monks are willing to make some concessions to expediency and continue to live on in the world, sharing, however, only in those activities which promise not to involve them in a compromise with what they believe is an essential and inviolable element of their code. They will not take life, or they will not lie. At some point they say: "Here I stand before an absolute; this is unconditionally forbidden." Like the man who announced he would never learn to drive an automobile for fear he might become involved in an accident and kill someone, at one stage they withdraw from the world to remain true to their code.

At their best the monk and the part-time monk play a constructive part in community life. They often represent a quality of living which by its attractive-

Dorothy Fosdick, "Ethical Standards and Political Strategies," *Political Science Quarterly*, 57 (1942), 214–228. Reprinted by permission.

ness condemns conventional practices and lifts the moral standards of a whole group. Moreover, their moral earnestness and continual concern for improving the quality of social relationships constantly lead to beneficial social practices. But these qualifications do not lessen certain unfortunate effects of their position on political strategy.

In the first place, they are unable to take full-time responsibility for political activity. The monk renounces responsibility for major political decisions altogether; the neo-monk accepts part-time responsibility up to the point where his essential rule of action is not violated, or is not likely to be violated. So the monk ignores the crucial political problems. Living in Utopian communities he comes to think in perfectionist terms and disregards the immediate problem of raising the level of conditions in society as a whole. He plays no part in the making of political decisions, and it is possible that his very neutrality on those matters may in fact encourage a course of events which leads to conditions that are worse than before.

On the other hand, the quasi-monk continues to participate in political decisions, but is prepared to disassociate himself from political movements the moment a decision is called for that would cause him to transgress his a priori rule. If he holds a position of leadership he may call off a movement entirely, as Gandhi did in the First Civil Disobedience campaign in India. More probably, like the pacifist George Lansbury on the eve of the Abyssinian conflict, he will resign his leadership and turn over a political party to the guidance of others. Or like William Jennings Bryan, when the United States went to war in 1917, he will surrender his responsible position in the government. No matter how seri-

ous the effects upon his cause he abides by his code. So from the beginning he puts his cause at the mercy of the opposition, particularly if he has widely circulated his scruples. Knowing there is one line of action which will not be taken, an hostile group can create circumstances which make that line of action unavoidable. The movement must then be abandoned, or its leadership must resign. Fortunately, even quasi-monks do not always act consistently, for Gandhi refused to call off the Second Civil Disobedience campaign when sporadic acts of violence occurred among his followers.

More serious still, however, is a second result which follows from the literal application of an absolute ethic. In so far as the monk and quasi-monk deal with political problems, they cannot handle them objectively. They approach most problems with a preconceived idea of what ought to be done. Convinced of the a priori rightness of one alternative, they do not consider frankly the social consequences that may be involved in it. They tend to adopt a strategy without regard for its effects. So the purist of "international law" believes his country should strictly observe the rules, no matter what another country does, or what the consequences. So absolute pacifists do not sanction the use of violence or the initiation of moves which might culminate in violence, even when to refuse to do so quite clearly increases the amount of violence that must ultimately break out. In Germany during the early twenties they did not support the proposal to form a republican army composed of people whose deepest interests would have led them to maintain the Republic against the threats of tyranny, so Hitler came safely to power. In May 1933 they did not encourage England to join with France in intervening in Germany to prevent her rearming, so Hitler was able to start what promises to be the most disastrous of all wars. While the part-time monks are not by any means altogether responsible for the turn of events, they are in part responsible; for in periods of crisis their action tends to be defensive rather than objective. They are apt to avoid facing the consequences of their decisions, for fear of being shaken in their a priori judgments. So often they are more concerned to safeguard their moral position than to improve the objective situation, like some absolute pacifists, who today spend greater energy in avoiding participation in violence than in doing what they can to increase the possibilities of a just peace. There is of course the other type of absolute pacifist thoroughly committed to the task of building a better world by non-violent methods. It is likely that men who resist all war hysteria will be able to devote their attention to the needs of a peace settlement with greater objectivity than those who have been primarily concerned with getting military victory. Some pacifists make this the utilitarian justification of their position. On the other hand, it is also probable that the judgment of a pacifist regarding postwar political organization will remain warped by his irrevocable opposition to certain political methods.

As long as the monk and the part-time monk comprise only a small portion of a population, they do not seriously imperil the chances of getting an adequate strategy. Indeed, there is a good deal to be said for the medieval notion of dividing moral responsibilities between different vocations in the population, so that a few very good monks compensate in part for the ordinary run of sinner. On condition that they are not too numerous, monks and part-time monks may in fact have certain positive effects upon political strategy. Resignations and martyrdoms are perennially necessary techniques of protest against both minority and majority decisions, and it is still the absolutist who is most likely to make the requisite protest. In the long run a Quaker's refusal to compromise with the war system is probably more politically valuable than his positive participation in any war effort, especially since he may be temperamentally unfitted for the latter role. Furthermore, the sharp line drawn by absolutists between action informed by principle and action arising from mere expediency may force our statesmen to reflect on the moral issues involved in their political decisions. A functional group of Quakers or Jehovah's Witnesses, by reason of their example, can help prevent statesmen from altogether renouncing moral considerations in politics. Today, however, Quaker fellow-travellers are no small minority of our population. Moreover, as a result of the democratic trend, most of them do not disassociate themselves from politics to pursue a saintly vocation or to preserve alive moral convictions to which they believe the world must some day return. Rather, as Elton Trueblood described them: "Their characteristic action is to try to manipulate a postal card barrage on Washington; their characteristic speech is the reference to the crisis as 'the President's War.'" When neo-monks flourish in large numbers, there is grave danger that their overscrupulous reservations will bedevil the political task.

To the second class of men who start with the assumption of an absolute ethic belong our modern Machiavellians and our neo-Machiavellians. They believe they violate a priori rules of right conduct every day of their lives. They may be able to avoid violence or lying in their private and intimate relations, but in their public relations they find themselves inescapably involved in unrighteousness. They therefore acknowledge that an absolute ethic is inapplicable to the tasks of politics. Since the only ethic for the pure Machiavellians is this absolute one, they abjure ethics altogether in their political dealings. Agreeing with their famous master that right and wrong have nothing to do with politics, they concern themselves with the success of their schemes and not their moral quality. The neo-Machiavellians, on the other hand, invent a special kind of ethic to apply in political matters which, unlike the absolute ethic, is expressed in adjustable rules of behavior. While they agree with the pure Machiavellians that no political acts are right, they maintain that some acts are *relatively* better than others. The relative worth of a choice is to be measured by its contribution to certain explicit political ends such as social order or social justice.

The advantages of a Machiavellian position in dealing with political tasks are obvious. Both the Machiavellian and the neo-Machiavellian give themselves wholeheartedly to political activity in a way not open to either the monk or the part-time monk. Furthermore, they are able to meet political crises with far greater objectivity and flexibility. Unimpeded by the concern to adhere strictly to a rule of proper action, they are free to consider the social consequences of their policies, and to mold those policies accordingly. Yet their position, also, has its calamitous effects upon political strategy.

In the first place, they usually content themselves with the conventional patterns of political behavior. The Machiavellian takes to current practices, no matter what their quality, without qualm of conscience; the neo-Machiavellian takes to them also, though with some misgivings. The Machiavellian does nothing to raise the level of political strategy. While continuing to be optimistic about the possibilities of improving the quality of his personal relations he becomes pessimistic and defeatist about political behavior. "For the manner in which men live is so different from the way in which they ought to live, that he who leaves the common course for that which he ought to follow will find that it leads him to ruin rather than to safety." In the attainment as well as in the maintenance of power the modern Machiavellian justifies any strategy. He makes violence normative, commonly advocating the final extermination of his enemies. In the guise of a patriot he calls for the deliberate killing of non-combatant enemy women in order to bring the war home to their husbands, and for "the wiping out of every last German."

On the other hand, while the neo-Machiavellian is not an outright cynic regarding the possibilities of improving the quality of political behavior, his position easily generates a similar defeatism. For he substitutes the goal of social justice or order for the Machiavellian principle of power, and justifies whatever is necessary to promote that end. The quality of the end he is after makes a good deal of difference to the strategies he adopts. So a modern Lutheran, who believes social order and peace are the highest political goals, advocates submission to the Hitler tyranny rather than non-violent resistance or war. Or a Christian Socialist, who believes social justice is the more worthy goal, advocates resistance to that tyranny no matter if it does mean war. The danger here, however, is not that passive submission or overt violence may at times be advocated, but that no tests are recognized by which some strategies are explicitly discouraged because of their devastating social consequences. With the absolute ethic defined as an impossibility the neo-Machiavellian chooses whichever among current practices promises to work. He is apt to be more contrite than the pure Machiavellian because he acknowledges that his political decisions are inevitably wrong. "For the good that I would I do not: but the evil which I would not, that I do." However, the assertion that no acts are right may not only encourage humility, but may produce the less wholesome reaction aptly expressed in the limerick:

In the classroom, when teacher had quit it,
A student said, now I have hit it,
Since nothing is right
I must find out tonight
The best sin to commit, and commit it.

A second consequence of the position taken by the Machiavellians and neo-Machiavellians is no less unfortunate. They tend not simply to accept conventional political practices, but they also tend to discourage the improvement of the ends of strategy. The pure Machiavellian eliminates all ethical considerations not only in selecting his means but also in choosing his objectives. He takes for granted that achieving political power is unconditionally worth while, and dismisses any criterion for testing that aim in relation to others. In contrast to the monk who urges obedience to an absolute *rule* of conduct, the Machiavellian thus advocates loyalty to an absolute *objective* of conduct, a position which has its special perils. For if no ethical principle is recognized as a guide

in selecting political objectives, their choice remains a wholly arbitrary matter. Moreover, the a priori selection of power as an aim is singularly capricious, since power is a neutral condition that can be used to promote any cause. A single-hearted devotion to the task of making America strong may in the long run assure the collapse of Hitler's tyranny, but it may also produce a new and devastating democratic imperialism. The Machiavellian is not merely helpless in forestalling this outcome but he even tends to encourage it. Admitting no principle in terms of which he can criticize and reject the baser objectives of power, he supports a strong America, no matter what it does. While the monk typically distinguishes himself by an overcritical attitude toward every political movement, the Machiavellian characteristically follows the crowd, shouting "America, right or wrong."

On the other hand, the neo-Machiavellian may make an effort to retain the absolute ethic as a principle of discriminate criticism between the ends of political strategy. He may, for example, use the commandment of love as a guide in selecting social justice rather than social order as a political goal. But the practice of using an absolute ethic as a criterion of criticism encourages another result. Being convinced that the ethic to love your neighbor as yourself has never been and can never be applied in politics, the common run of neo-Machiavellian easily ignores it altogether, thus losing not merely a rule of conduct but also a criterion for testing ends of action. He may rescue an ethical criterion with which to measure the relative merits of alternative ends by redefining the absolute ethic as an ideal or principle of criticism. If such a redefinition takes place he avoids the worst perils of the Machiavellian position, for, in the light of that principle, he can discard some objectives of strategy as unworthy. This explains why the neo-Machiavellian at his best is often the convinced reformer: the Christian Socialist or the New Deal evangelist. If, as is so frequently the case, however, the redefinition does not take place, the neo-Machiavellian becomes as opportunistic and uncritical as the best of them.

When the Machiavellian and his fellow-travellers were confined to a ruling class or the entourage of a prince they were not so dangerous as their modern representatives. They could be ruthless on the stage of politics while most of the people quietly continued to preserve a more respectable morality. There could be a division of moral responsibility whereby the prince was a cruel fighter and his subjects humble and hard-working folk. But now the bulk of our people are politically active and many of them have discovered the secrets which once belonged only to their leaders. Under ancient tyrannies "robber morality" was held to be justified only in extreme cases and then solely for the ruling groups, but today, under fascist tyrannies, "robber morality" is publicly acknowledged to be proper for whole nations of men that are striving for status. In more democratic states waging modern war, increasing numbers of common men and women are tempted to see violence not merely as an unfortunate last resort but as the norm of all political behavior. When the Machiavellian and the neo-Machiavellian are as plentiful among us as they already are today, their patent cynicism may finally corrupt our political task.

The primary difficulty with the position of both the monk and the Machiavellian is their initial assumption of an absolute ethic; for the belief that rules of conduct are unconditionally right or wrong involves the confusion of two distinct ideas: the good and the right. The good is what is worth while for its own sake, what a man conceives to be of unqualified value. There are things good in themselves which a man enjoys here and now on their own account, if he is not to be forever caught in the pursuit of means. There is also the good which he believes ultimately desirable, the love of God, peace, truth, or beauty. However the good is defined, and on whatever level of experience, it has the quality of being worth while as an end in itself. The right on the other hand is the best way of promoting the good. It is the choice among available alternatives which is most likely to further the final value. To one it is a service to his neighbor, to another a diligent effort to develop non-violent techniques of resistance to evil, to still others a long and arduous research task, or the painting of a picture. These activities are not right in themselves, but only in so far as they promote what is considered ultimately desirable. A man thus derives his idea of the right from his conception of the *summum bonum*. The common mistake of the monk, the part-time monk, the Machiavellian and the neo-Machiavellian is to identify these two logically derivative ideas. They define the good as an ethical imperative. Whether they interpret the good as perfect disinterestedness, or peace, or truth, they call it an ethic of right action. One ought to be wholly disinterested, one ought to avoid all violence, one should tell the whole truth. They identify what they are ultimately after with what they believe ought to be done at the moment.

This identification of the good and the right gravely imperils the functions which these two ideas serve. The good is above all the criterion in terms of which right actions are distinguished from wrong. The right is the action one ought to choose among the possibilities which are open. The one is a criterion of value, the other an ethic of action. These two functions are what the neo-Machiavellian tries to provide for when he postulates two kinds of ethics; his absolute ethic serves in part as a criterion, while his interim political ethic indicates the relatively better choice among actual alternatives. But the position of the neo-Machiavellian is inadequate on two scores. In the first place, he wrongly attributes to a criterion the character of an ethic. The good is not an actual alternative of action. Opportunities do not present themselves to love perfectly, or to act wholly disinterestedly. It is impossible to escape indirect participation in the taking of life or the expression of partial truths. Even the highest-minded monk does not avoid implication in exploitation and violence, nor escape either passion or bias simply by thinking them away. While the neo-Machiavellian admits that an absolute ethic is universally violated in political life, he does not go far enough in admitting that such an ethic is never a choice in any relationship. If the good is then not an alternative of action, and yet, according to the neo-Machiavellian, it is right to choose the good, everything we do is wrong. When the impossible becomes an ethic, we are put forever in a position where nothing we can do is right. The only logical conclusion of the matter is that there are no ethics at all.

In avoiding this disastrous inference the neo-Machiavellian falls into a second error. He proposes to leave personal concerns to the jurisdiction of his absolute ethic while recognizing a special political ethic made up of adjust-able rules of action. In fact, however, such adaptable rules constitute the only sort of ethic that exists in any sphere of experience. There are not two kinds of ethics, an absolute one for one sphere and a relative one for another; there is only a relative ethic. For in all actual situations, rules of conduct clash with one another, and we must continuously choose between them. Shall we protect the naughty child sought by his father by hiding the truth of his whereabouts or shall we tell his whereabouts and be responsible for his punishment? Shall we practice non-violence, and let a neighboring nation be destroyed, or shall we attack first and preserve its independence? Shall we send an Expeditionary Force to Europe and thereby lose large numbers of young Americans in an effort to shorten the war, or shall we withhold such a force while the war is prolonged and more Europeans are killed? Given limited alternatives of decision, we cannot escape weighing one rule against another and choosing whichever alternative seems the best solution of the dilemma. There is no difference in this respect between a man deciding which of two girls he is going to ask to marry him, and a statesman deciding between alternative strategies. Some pragmatic pacifists, disassociating themselves from their absolute brethren, claim that participation by the United States in war is wrong, because the effects of war are more disastrous than the results of refusing to fight. Whatever the wisdom of their judgment, they justifiably hold that the rightness or wrongness of a strategy depends upon its social consequences.

Any way one approaches the matter, a basis for wise political strategy is difficult to arrive at, unless one starts with a clear distinction between the good and the right.

In what situation, then, do we find ourselves when we make this distinction and thus deny an absolute ethic as the basis of our conduct? The monk would have us believe that on that account our actions become unprincipled. But certainly this does not follow. We must bear in mind the difference between an absolute ethic viewed as a system of specific rules considered right in themselves and an absolute value held to be good in itself and therefore unqualifiedly worth working for. While we reject the system of rules, we can at the same time affirm the validity of a universal value as the ultimate criterion for our practical choices. We can acknowledge an ideal good beyond the partial values of political life, and thus recognize a universal standard for discriminating between goals and means of strategy. So, avowing the ultimate worth and dignity of human personality, we can pledge ourselves to the creation of conditions where every person will be able to develop freely to his fullest capacity. While, in the light of this value, no political objective is unqualifiedly worth while nor any tactic categorically right, some objectives become more worth while than others and tactics which are most likely to promote those objectives become right. The terms "right" and "wrong" are then not merely convenient variants for "expedient" and "inexpedient," "successful" and "unsuccessful." They refer to those strategies which show promise of promoting conditions where every man, woman and child can live according to his own highest ideals.

In practice this means two things. In the first place, political goals are tested to discover those which promise to be most conducive to the good. The validity of a choice cannot be finally proved, but its significance can be checked on

the basis of experience. So we select the objective of social justice and not merely social order, since order may be based on an exploiting tyranny. We aim for equal economic opportunity and not economic liberty, since the latter may allow a few to monopolize the limited opportunities of life. In the second place, intermediate norms of conduct are formulated to serve as guides in choosing the means to these objectives. These norms include what experience indicates on the whole promotes the good: respect for the plighted word, the treatment of men as ends and not as means, acknowledgment of the solidarity of all nations and races, and the equal claim of all to share in the chances of life. Strategy is not slavishly bound to these principles, but they are taught and used as leads in selecting practices that violate as little as possible the final good. So if violence is necessary as a final resort to keep open the channels for increasing justice, we do not altogether shrink from it, but we normally advocate non-violent tactics to promote justice because such tactics do not destroy life.

The neo-Machiavellians commonly charge that the denial of an absolute ethic, and the consequent admission that some actions are right, inevitably encourages self-righteous and therefore ruthless action. But this also is by no means necessarily the case. The ideal good to which we are committed can never be wholly actualized, and therefore stands not merely as a criterion of choice but also as a principle of judgment on all our achievements. Some actions are right because they are the best choice we can make between limited alternatives. But they do not represent a fulfillment of the good. Indeed, we recognize that even a right action never unqualifiedly promotes the good, for results may follow that delay or undermine existing approximations of the final value. So participation in war may not only destroy an unjust tyranny but it may also bring down the democratic structures through which we hoped to work in building a juster peace. John Bennett put the matter well in saying: "War is never good because it is always primarily destructive of values. It may be right in those circumstances in which it is the only way of preventing a greater evil." There is much to be said for the humility produced by the neo-Machiavellian tension between the right he believes he ought to do, and the wrong he actually succeeds in doing. But this way of stating the matter involves too sharp a distinction between an absolute right and relative wrongs. There is the truer tension which can be as effective in checking our pride and can be far more effective in encouraging us to improve our ways. It is the tension between the good we finally hope for and the poor approximations we actually accomplish.

The view of morality presented in these pages does not necessarily promote agreement on current matters of political decision. If morality involves taking a whole situation into account and choosing whatever action is most likely to forward the good, some will disagree with our definition of the good, and many will differ with our judgment of right action. Yet the fact remains that this view of morality is the indispensable minimum foundation of an adequate political strategy. On the one hand, it secures us from approaching the political task with a preconceived idea of what ought to be done. Strategies are selected on the basis of their probable results, not their self-evident value. Moves in the war are discussed in terms of alternatives which will tend to further what we are finally after, not in terms of a priori judgments about the use of violence. On the other hand, this conception of morality also saves us from rejecting considerations of right and wrong in making our political judgments, or inventing a special kind of ethic to avoid this outcome. Political decisions are treated like other decisions, only with the awareness that greater values usually depend upon them. Statesmen and citizens, no less than private persons in their intimate relationships, are held responsible for taking the total situation into the focus of consciousness to choose the best alternative that is open to them. Only if we are thus fortified against both the too-righteous reservations of the monk, and the cynical excesses of the Machiavellian, can we confront responsibly the momentous political tasks of our generation.

Suggestions for Additional Reading

A very interesting way to approach the problem of the Compromise of 1850 is to read the interpretations of some of the leading writers in the American historiographical tradition. It is interesting to compare the analyses of the crisis and the assessments of the roles of political leaders in such older works as: Hermann Von Holst, *The Constitutional and Political History of the United States*, III, IV (Chicago, 1881); James Schouler, *History of the United States of America*, Vol. V (New York, 1891); James Ford Rhodes, *History of the United States From the Compromise of 1850*, I (New York, 1892); John B. Mac-Master, *History of the People of the United States*, VIII; Edward Channing, *A History of the United States*, VI (New York, 1925). This investigation of the great works of historical synthesis in American historiography should include a distinguished representative of our own generation, Allan Nevins, whose *Ordeal of the Union*, 2 vols. (New York, 1947), uses much modern scholarship for this period of our history.

Other recent studies of the political history of the 1840's and 1850's containing much useful material for an understanding of the events preceding and succeeding the Compromise of 1850 are: Fredrick Jackson Turner, *The United States, 1830–1850* (New York, 1935), especially the later chapters; Arthur M. Schlesinger, Jr., *The Age of Jackson* (Boston, 1945), the last four chapters; Avery Craven, *The Coming of the Civil War* (New York, 1942); and for good background material on social and cultural forces, Arthur Cole, *The Irrepres-*

sible Conflict 1860–1865 (New York, 1936). See also a much neglected work by Milo M. Quaife, *The Doctrine of Non-Intervention with Slavery in the Territories* (Chicago, 1910).

For studies of party organization and internal party politics consult such works as: Roy F. Nichols, *The Democratic Machine, 1850–54* (New York, 1923); George R. Poage, *Henry Clay and the Whig Party* (Chapel Hill, 1936); Arthur C. Cole, *The Whig Party in the South* (Washington, 1913); Glyndon Van Deusen, *Thurlow Weed, Wizard of the Lobby* (Boston, 1947); F. H. Hodder, "Authorship of the Compromise of 1850," *Mississippi Valley Historical Review*, XXII (March, 1936), 525–36. A very good article on Senatorial politics which also contains some provocative ideas on the historiography of the Compromise is Holman Hamilton's "Democratic Senate Leadership and the Compromise of 1850," *Mississippi Valley Historical Review*, XLI (December, 1954), 403–418.

There is much good writing about the South during this period. Particularly valuable for understanding the mind of the South are W. J. Cash, *The Mind of the South* (New York, 1941) and Jesse T. Carpenter, *The South as a Conscious Minority, 1789–1861* (New York, 1930). Special studies of southern behavior at the time of the compromise are numerous: Chauncey S. Boucher, "The Secession and Cooperation Movements in South Carolina, 1848 to 1852," *Washington University Studies*, V, No. 2 (April, 1918), 65–138; Cleo Hearon, *Mississippi and the Compromise of 1850* (Oxford, Miss., 1913); Richard H. Shryock,

Georgia and the Union in 1850 (Durham, N. C., 1926); Philip Ray Hamer, *Secession Movement in South Carolina, 1847–1852* (Allentown, Pa., 1918); St. George L. Sioussat, "Tennessee, the Compromise of 1850, and the Nashville Convention," *Mississippi Valley Historical Review*, II (December, 1915), 313–47; Lewey Dorman, *Party Politics in Alabama from 1850 through 1860* (Montgomery, Ala., 1935); Melvin J. White, "Louisiana and the Secession Movement of the Early Fifties," Mississippi Valley Historical Association, *Proceedings*, VIII, 278; Herbert J. Doherty, Jr., "Florida and the Crisis of 1850," *Journal of Southern History*, XIX (February, 1953), 32–47.

Studies which deal with attitudes and behavior in other sections besides the South should also be consulted. See the relevant chapters in such books as: Philip S. Foner, *Business and Slavery* (Chapel Hill, 1941); Russel B. Nye, *Fettered Freedom, Civil Liberties and the Slavery Controversy, 1830–1860* (East Lansing, Mich., 1949); Russel B. Nye, *William Lloyd Garrison and the Humanitarian Reformers* (Boston, 1955); Ralph Korngold, *Two Friends of Man* (Boston, 1950); Ralph L. Rusk, *The Life of Ralph Waldo Emerson* (New York, 1949). Consult also H. D. Foster's article, "Webster's Seventh of March Speech," *American Historical Review*, XXVII (January, 1922), 245–270. For the full flavor of the bitter reaction to Webster's speech and the Compromise of 1850 by anti-slavery intellectuals in the North, read John Greenleaf Whittier's "Ichabod" and Ralph Waldo Emerson's speech on "The Fugitive Slave Law" in any edition of these writers' works.

Two useful articles on the political situation in New York are: Harry J. Carman and Reinhard H. Luthin, "The Seward-Fillmore Feud and the Crisis of 1850," *New York History*, XXIV (April, 1943), 163–184 and, by the same authors in the same volume, 335–357, "The Seward-Filmore Feud and the Disruption of the Whig Party." An excellent chapter on Illinois and the Compromise appears in Arthur Cole's volume in the Centennial History of Illinois, *Eve of the Civil War* (Springfield, Ill., 1919); see also George D. Harmon, "Douglas and the Compromise of 1850," *Journal of the Illinois State Historical Society*, XXI (January, 1929), 453–499. For one aspect of the southwestern territorial problem, see William Campbell Binkley's "The Question of Texan Jurisdiction in New Mexico under the United States, 1848–1850," *Southwestern Historical Quarterly*, XXIV (July, 1920), 1–38.

Biographical resources are enormous for this period. Among other works consult Glyndon Van Deusen, *The Life of Henry Clay* (Boston, 1937); Claude Fuess, *Daniel Webster*, 2 vols. (Boston, 1930); Charles M. Wiltse, *John C. Calhoun, Sectionalist, 1840–1850* (New York, 1951); Frederick Bancroft, *The Life of William H. Seward*, 2 vols. (New York, 1900); George F. Milton, *The Eve of Conflict, Stephen A. Douglas and a Needless War* (Boston, 1934); Holman Hamilton, *Zachary Taylor, Soldier in the White House* (New York, 1951); Frank B. Woodford, *Lewis Cass, The Last Jeffersonian* (New Brunswick, N.J., 1950); William Ernest Smith, *The Francis Preston Blair Family in Politics* (New York, 1933).

Since political speeches in this period were of a very high order, students should consult available editions of the collected works of Calhoun, Clay, Seward, Webster, and also Thomas Hart Benton's *Thirty Years' View*. The *Con-*

gressional Globe for the sessions of the 31st Congress makes more exciting reading than many would suspect. Finally, no student should miss a chance to read whatever newspapers are available in his library for the period 1848–1852 and also such outstanding political journals as *The United States Magazine and Democratic Review,* and *The American Whig Review.*